The Geopolitics of Information

The Geopolitics of Information

HOW WESTERN CULTURE DOMINATES
THE WORLD

by
ANTHONY SMITH

OXFORD UNIVERSITY PRESS
New York

OXFORD UNIVERSITY PRESS

Oxford   London   Glasgow
New York   Toronto   Melbourne   Wellington
Nairobi   Dar es Salaam   Cape Town
Kuala Lumpur   Singapore   Jakarta   Hong Kong   Tokyo
Delhi   Bombay   Calcutta   Madras   Karachi

First published in the United States by Oxford University Press, New York, 1980
First issued as an Oxford University Press paperback, New York, 1981

The Library of Congress has cataloged this publication as follows:

Smith, Anthony, 1938-
    The geopolitics of information: how Western culture
    dominates the world/by Anthony Smith. — New York: Oxford
    University Press, 1980.

    192 p.; 23 cm.

    Includes bibliographical references and index.
    ISBN 0-19-520208-2
    ISBN 0-19-520274-0 (pbk.)

1. Communication, International.   2. World politics —
1975-1985.   3. Cultural relations.   I. Title.

P96.I5S6   1980   80-80560
                                                          MARC

P
96
I 5
S 6
1981

This printing: 9 8 7
Printed in the United States of America

Dedicated to four teachers and friends:

JAY BLUMLER

ASA BRIGGS

HILDE HIMMELWEIT

ELIHU KATZ

There stands my model, then: fearless, incorruptible, independent, a believer in frankness and veracity; one that will call a spade a spade, make no concession to likes and dislikes, nor spare any man for pity or respect or propriety: an impartial judge, kind to all; but too kind to none; a literary cosmopolite with neither suzerain nor king, never heeding what this or that man may think, but setting down the thing that befell.

LUCIAN OF SAMOSATA
from 'The Way to Write History'

Every country is held at some time to account for the windows broken by its press; the bill is presented, some day or other, in the shape of hostile sentiment in the other country.

BISMARCK

Si je lâche la bride à la presse, je ne resterai pas trois mois au pouvoir.

NAPOLEON

It is now beginning to be felt that journalism is to modern Europe what political oratory was to Athens and Rome, and that, to become what it ought, it should be wielded by the same sort of men.

JOHN STUART MILL

The objectives of the press: to understand the popular feeling and give expression to it; another is to arouse among the people certain desirable sentiments; the third is fearlessly to expose popular defects.

MAHATMA GANDHI

I abhor censorship.   INDIRA GANDHI

Contents

Preface

A crisis is a condition of instability leading towards a decisive change. This book deals with a crisis.

In the early years after the Second World War, the globe seemed to divide between 'East' and 'West', corresponding to the great ideological and economic divisions between the socialist- and capitalist-leaning nations. In later decades, however, it became clear that another great divide was being superimposed upon this, a divide between 'North' and 'South', between the prosperous developing nations (which include many socialist societies) and the struggling developing nations of the former empires which seemed to be predominantly in the equatorial zones and southern hemisphere. Hence a North–South dialogue seems to have stolen the limelight from the East–West tensions of the Cold War period.

Recently, the disposition of power in the world has been slowly tilting away from the countries of the North. The failure of American policy in South-East Asia, the oil crisis, the collapse of the Shah's regime, along with many other processes and events, have served to increase the confidence of the leaders of the Third or developing World in their growing *collective* political authority, even though the economic gap between the rich and poor nations of the world has continued to widen. The result has been that the Northern countries have been placed under increasing pressure to adjust their trading and industrial policies to the greater advantage of the Southern nations.

At the same time, a parallel pressure has been exerted in the field of information, where a number of international agencies, notably UNESCO, have become the forum for a growing controversy since the middle of the decade. The Third World has accused the West of cultural domination through its control of the major news-collecting resources of the world, through the unstinted flow of its cultural products across the world, and through the financial power of its advertising agencies, its international newspaper chains, its newsprint companies and its hold over the electro-magnetic spectrum on which broadcasting, navigation, meteorology and much else depend. The swamping effect of this vast machinery has transformed the social fabric of Third World countries as it has repressed its traditional cultures. Above all, the South has complained of the fact that the four major wire services or news agencies of the world (Reuters, Agence France-Presse, United Press International and the Associated Press) belong to three nations but supply 90 per cent of the international news which passes into the world's newsrooms.

The Report of the UNESCO committee of 'fifteen wise men and one woman' specially appointed by Secretary General M'Bow under the chairmanship of Sean MacBride,[1] has now brought the controversy to a new stage. For the better part of two years this committee was a major focus for research reports and propagandist speeches and papers. It has attempted to 'settle' a wide range of political, philosophical and professional problems concerning the reporting of the affairs of the developing world in the developed and vice versa, and to do so in a manner which is acceptable to the different competing ideologies of the world. The legacy of the MacBride Commission will inevitably be a continuation of the debate and its general 'invasion' into the whole sphere of international relations. This is no bad thing for the question of information now lies at the heart of the world economy and cannot be separated from the other conflicts and issues of which international and national politics are composed.

At the heart of the controversy in its present form lies a delicate moral or philosophical conundrum. The Western nations share, to different degrees and with different results, a common belief in the separation of power between the press (including radio and television) and government. The adherence to a privately owned and 'free' press is indeed perhaps the one fully shared *self-defining* belief of the democratic West. It is an intellectual doctrine but also an economic precept, part and parcel of the notion of laissez-faire. In developing societies, so it is argued, the machinery of government is so frail and so unstable that the constant winds of change generated by a free press would make political and social settlement impossible. The socialist world shares a different doctrine, though a similar practice, to that of many capitalist developing societies: it functions on the assumption that the press must only present information consistent with the society's acknowledged goals. A dull propagandist uniformity envelops the socialist media. Even Mr Brezhnev has argued that this has been taken too far, making the Soviet media too unresponsive to public taste. None the less, in many of the international gatherings at which the information issue has been discussed, the socialist representatives have insisted upon the correctness of the attack of the developing societies upon Western information doctrines. On the other hand, the developing world's spokesmen have not always supported the position of the socialist camp, which has itself often been accused of its own version of cultural domination. The Third World has, throughout this debate, attempted to work out a separate doctrine of its own, and it is the Third World position, rather than the doctrine of the socialist countries, which has more successfully struck out at the West, where Soviet press theory and practice are held in an unswerving repugnance, depriving them of significant influence.

The conflict between North and South over the dissemination of news is more intractable than any other contemporary debate over the unfair distribution of earth resources, for it intrudes into the very culture of Western societies. It is argued that the mass audience of the industrialized world has become conditioned to a view of the non-industrialized world which is in itself exploitative, patronizing, distorted; that that audience is so powerful an agent in itself over the international machinery which gathers and shapes information that its appetite for 'wrong' or ill-judged information about the Third World is self-feeding, self-sustaining. The agencies provide a diet of news which they believe their client newspapers and magazines will publish and they, in turn, provide that which they believe their audiences will relish. Famine, disorder, corruption, disruption are the common topics. If the publication of the resulting material is then damaging to the interests of the developing nations in their search for capital, for markets, for a just share of world resources, it is arguable that the blame must be directed at those institutions which condition the mass mind of the West. Thus, in the international forums, set up to examine such questions, pressure has come to be exerted upon Western governments to do the very thing which the doctrines of the West themselves forbid—to interfere in the control and content of the press.

The debate has had its negative aspects in the Third World countries themselves. In heaping blame upon the Western media, these governments have constructed fake justification for their own domestic repressions of journalism. The debate has largely been held between governments, rather than between governments and journalists. Even where journalists willingly subject their craft to the developmental needs of their societies, they have nevertheless still found themselves at loggerheads with their governments. Freedom is something that journalists need, *everywhere*. They require freedom from restraints of both the market-place and government;

both lead towards the distortion of information. Thus, those who cry for 'balance' in the world flow of information have come to aid the processes by which information in some societies is deliberately constrained, while those who cry for 'freedom' in the flow of information may well, in certain market conditions, be aiding the processes which lead to distortion and injustice. It is a double crisis, intractable both in doctrine and in management.

The controversy has provided the Third World with a certain political leverage, since the information industries are now an important sector of many Western economies. In challenging the universal efficacy of the doctrine of press freedom the spokesmen of the former group have forced the information issue beyond the half-closed doors of international conferences and the completely closed doors of American, Western European and Japanese corporations. As a result of such pressure the affairs of the Third World may come to be reported with greater care, while journalists, editors, publishers and governments are being forced to contemplate again the meaning of their mutual duties and responsibilities. Though the accusations against Western journalism may have been overplayed, it is unlikely that the press of the West will become less 'free' as a result of the fracas. Rather the reverse. It may force a revaluation of the condition of freedom alongside a reconsideration of press ethics.

The collecting, editing and distribution of information is now a key element in all economies. It is not inaptly that the French have come to speak of the 'informatisation' of society;[2] more and more governmental, economic and cultural processes have come to depend upon a set of companies, institutions and systems which make up the information sector and so the tension over the international flow of news has spread across a wide range of concerns which formerly were not conceived as part of this sector. Changing technology has brought more and more matters into the problem-strewn area of information policy, now subject to this further international wrangle. The purpose of this essay is to describe the various lines along which the controversy has been growing and point out some possible future points of synthesis or agreement. Nothing further than that is proposed. One should not speak of 'solutions', for the problem is not a mathematical one. It is but one aspect of the whole problem of international domination, inequality and dependence.

This book arose from an idea of Jack Glattbach, the editor of *Populi*, and Tarzie Vittachi, of the United Nations Fund for Population Activities, himself a former Third World newspaper editor who has written often on the same topic. The project was made financially viable through the efforts of Tarzie Vittachi and Jack Raymond at the Epoch B Foundation in New York, and of Erskine Childers at the United Nations Development Programme. I wish to thank Judith Acton for some diligent weeks of research work, Professor Albert Pickerell at the University of California at Berkeley for valuable advice and Father Michael Traber of the World Association for Christian Communication (WACC) for patient effort on my behalf. I have held important conversations for which I wish to offer thanks, with all of the above, and also with Chen Chimutengwende, Christopher Nascimento, Godwin Matatu, Wilson Dizard, John Howkins, Asher Deleon, Stanley Swinton, Robert Manoff, Henry Gathigira, Kenneth Best, Hilary Ng'weno, Joe Rodrigues, James Kangwana, Richard Sakala, Donald Baptiste, Kenneth Jowett, Mehra Masani, Pran Chopra, Tiny Chatterjee, Krishna Raj, Hamdy Kandil, Einar Östgaard, Chakravarthi Raghavan, Jonathan Gunter, Klaus Knipping, Jean Roussel. Needless to say, all errors and misjudgements are my own. I must thank Yvonne Cleall for making a fine job of a difficult manuscript in record time. Matthew Evans, Managing Director of Faber and Faber, has been an extraordinarily prompt and encouraging publisher. Eddi Ploman performed a most thorough reading of the manuscript, bringing many errors to light. Timothy O'Grady edited the manuscript with an admirable meticulousness.

1. The Old International Information Order

I

For five centuries explorers, geographers, cartographers, colonists, travellers, adventurers, warriors and reporters have attempted to describe in different ways and for different reasons unfamiliar regions of the planet. Most of them have come from the nations of the West. Until Columbus returned from his voyage across the Atlantic, the continent of Europe was an island in the unknown; signals, rumours and confused memories constantly reached it from other lands to the north, south, east and west, which in the mind of the West were long the stuff of legend and of dream, the lure of lonely and curious and avaricious voyagers, a constant temptation to those among the learned who had read of a more complex, many-shored but interlocking world which had existed in classical times.

In the first century, a pilot named Hippalus had worked out a navigational technique for sailing right across the open sea,[1] by which means the lands of the Mediterranean were able to open up regular shipping routes to India and beyond. Until that time sailing had involved a permanent hugging of coastlines, a fact which provides some explanation for the misconceptions which lay at the root of the geography and cartography of the Middle Ages. The Indian Ocean was deemed by Ptolemy to be a vast lake on the model of the Mediterranean, and later journeys merely helped to reinterpret rather than displace the Ptolemaic system until the end of the fifteenth century.[2]

There have survived a number of maps of the world drawn in the fourteenth century and earlier which describe in plentiful detail the peoples dwelling on continents which remained unexplored or even undiscovered until much more recent times. There is a great deal to be learned about European societies from these undaunted efforts in reporting on the unknown.[3] One such *mappemonde* found in a copy of Higden's *Polychronicon* marks the lands of the Androphagi who eat one another, the Garamentes who live in a zone where the water boils by day and freezes by night, the Farici who live on the raw flesh

of panthers, the Monoculi who possess one leg apiece but who none
the less can run very fast and who spend their days sitting benignly
in the sun with their single foot held as a sunshade above them
(indeed a map held in Hereford Cathedral provides a useful picture).
There were also the Virgogici who eat insects, the Troglodytes
who eat serpents, the Antipodes who have sixteen fingers and practise
a form of ecstatic dance. There was one nation whose heads grew
beneath their shoulders, another with umbrella lips, one without
tongues, one without noses, one without ears. There were clearly
marked the precise areas inhabited by the Gorgons, the Dragons
and sea-monsters and one place—'*hic sirene habundant*'—where
sirens dwelt in plenty.

This phantasmagoria of ethnography was slow to melt away from
the maps of post-Renaissance, empirically minded Europe. It had
taken centuries to accumulate and even in the seventeenth century
there were respectable cartographers still using Pliny and Herodotus
as authorities for the locations of some of these oddly designed races.
The travellers of a thousand years had as often added to the number
of phantom continents and apparitional peoples as they had de-
tracted from them; even Christopher Columbus, according to an
account left us by one of his sons, saw a mermaid or two on his way
to America. Persistent voyaging eventually caused the monsters to
fade away, however, into the mundane shapes of apes, gorillas and
other fauna. The illusory creatures had been projections of mis-
understood realities; explorers tempted into the unknown waters of
Africa, Asia, South America and the antipodes by foreknowledge of
the uncanny found it extremely difficult to deny what others were
presumed to have seen. Half-remembered monsters continued to
haunt the minds of the map-makers, empire-builders and empire-
destroyers of the fifteenth and sixteenth centuries, and were only
crowded out of consciousness by the vastness of the palpable dis-
coveries of the age. After all, they had been sighted by honest men
who needed a good tale to tell and whose public needed its preconceptions confirmed by evidence.

For the people of the European lands and those who left them to
found new countries across the Atlantic and Pacific Oceans, the
indigenous peoples of Africa, Asia, and America grew out of this
phantasmagoria, dwelling as they had done in a vast region which
for centuries had lain on very early maps under the one-word rubric
'Brumae', the fogs which separated the tiny island of the known
world from the even more impenetrably severe zone of 'Gelidae',

which lay at the very rim of reality. Europe seemed to lie between an area to the north in which the elements were frozen into unmalleable solidity and one to the south where they remained permanently molten by fervent heat, between 'the icy breath of polar seas and the fiery noon of equatorial calms', as John Livingstone Lowes put it.[4] Each step the explorers took, each lifting of the mists entailed merging the unknown with the familiar, for such 'progress' revealed an alteration in the pattern of all nature and had to be assimilated into the previously known reality.

Thus it proceeded, until Bartholomeo Diaz was driven beyond the Cape and found there was no land joining Africa with India, that the Indian Ocean was after all no lake as portrayed in Ptolemaic geography, but an endless sheet of water. Then da Gama found his way to Calicut by crossing this impossible ocean in one bound to provide Europe with the task of absorbing a whole range of new peoples and cultures. Meanwhile, in the other direction, the Spaniards followed Columbus's route and by 1500 found their way to Brazil and the Argentine. Another great Cape loomed into view and within a further twenty years Magellan had circumnavigated it, braving the giants and devils which he reported to be there. Each voyage both shifted the locus of ultimate terror and made more complete the transition from traditional fantasy to the real, while each piece of settlement brought part of the new reality inside the familiar culture of the exploring societies. Exploration was a pursuit of *information* and each added unit of information filled in a troubling uncertainty about the nature of the world. For the nations of Europe it was not merely a revelation of new pieces of territory; it entailed a complete reversal of the cosmos. The explored world was one in which the sun itself reversed its round and the whole known earth swung round upon her axis as the strange regions were entered. The full terror of the experience was later caught by Coleridge in 'The Rime of the Ancient Mariner':

The Sun came up upon the left,
Out of the sea came he!
And he shone bright, and on the right
Went down into the sea.
Higher and higher every day,
Till over the mast at noon—

It took several centuries of battered ships and shattered illusions for the West to assimilate the shock, and to acquire the strength—

moral, physical and financial—with which to handle this newly available world. What the explorer did was add to the map of the world, while confirming previously delineated outlines. Thus, the world has come to be locked inexorably into the conceptual embrace of the West. From these mental habits arose the explorer's heir, the modern reporter, and the entire apparatus of the 'information order' which has dominated the political realities of the globe in the last century and a half.

The idea that certain forms of historical writing should constitute the special genre of 'news' dates from the era in which technology made it possible to disseminate written material within a concentrated population on a prompt and regular basis. News depended upon printing, upon the organization of a distribution system and upon a market (including a market for advertising). From the start of this genre, in the early seventeenth century, it has been clear that it posed special problems of truth, accuracy and perspective. It was seen that truth of detail, *veracity*, was not the same as general truth or complete truth; there have been editors vexed by the problems of presenting news ever since it became clear that, by its very industrial nature, news-writing was a *bureaucratic* process entailing a hierarchy of crafts and professions. 'Truth is the daughter of Time,' writes a newsman of the period of the English Civil War. 'Whoever undertakes to write news, sails up a narrow channell,' writes another. The periodic, repetitious nature of the news medium, the fact that its material is culled from different sources, all of them partial, the fact that the choice of material must be geared to the appetites of a market—'Gentle Reader, how comes it that nothing will please you? . . .' writes yet another English Civil War newsman[5]—the impossibility of confirming distant information and the difficulty in deciding the journalist's locus of intellectual balance are all ancient factors in the evolution of the controversy about news.

The problem of balance is as ancient as the task of reporting. Lucian of Samosata's thesis on the writing of history was really aimed at *newsmen*, even though the writers he was instructing in the second century were working as historians for posterity rather than for a journalistic public. The inherent imprecisions were as clear in this context as in the days when news and history-writing diverged and took different paths of development. Lucian stipulated:

Facts are not to be collected at haphazard, but with careful, laborious, repeated investigation; when possible, a man should have been present and seen for himself; failing that, he should prefer the disinterested account, selecting the informants least likely to diminish or magnify from partiality. And here comes the occasion for exercising the judgement in weighing probabilities.

The exhortations to conscientiousness raise rather than resolve the problems of fairness and of truth, however, as Lucian himself was aware.

The historian's position should now be precisely that of Zeus in Homer, surveying now the Mysians', now the Thracian horse-men's land. Even so he will survey how his own party (telling us what we looked like to him from his post of vantage), now the Persians, and yet again both at once if they come to blows. . . . All this, however, with moderation; a subject is not to be ridden to death; no neglect of proportion, no childish engrossment, but easy transitions. . . . He has to make of his brain a mirror, unclouded, right, and true of surface; then he will reflect events as they presented themselves to him, neither distorted, discoloured, nor variable.[6]

Recent improvements in the technology of reporting—short-hand, telegraphy, photography, microphones, satellites, profiles, interviews—have increased rather than simplified the theoretical problems of objectivity in the news. News has acquired a new and perhaps more powerful authority from the size and scope of its vast contemporary audience and from the way in which the business of government has come to focus upon the issues which journalism selects for salience and priority.

The nineteenth century foreign newspaper reporter or corres-pondent working in the popular press saw himself in a sense as the rightful heir of the great explorers; he looked at the world as his object, of which he and his civilization were the subjects. Indeed, much newspaper reporting was deeply involved in the problems of colonial and other conquest as the more powerful civilizations shared out the available regions of influence. War reporting in the late nineteenth century and throughout the twentieth has only helped further to entrench the imperial imagery which lies at the heart of Western journalism. All the novels of the last hundred years about journalism—from Henry James's *The Reverberator*,[7] to Evelyn Waugh's *Scoop*,[8] Kipling's *The Light that Failed*[9] and Meredith's *Diana of the Crossways*[10]—bring out the linkages between newspaper reporting and the many manifestations of social, military and political power. The journalist is sent somewhere, equipped with the right of ubiquitous trespass, to transpose some distant reality into the preconceptions of his own audience/society. The editor is the director of political reality, the reporter his myrmidon and in the relationship between the two of them and their audience lies a complete world-structure, an image of reality shaped according to their mutual needs and aspirations. Domestic news can frequently be modified through the experience of the reader, but audiences must accept reports from the reporter/historian of foreign wars and other events, for there is simply no substitute for him in society. Even more insidiously, such reports have to be rendered meaningful to readers who do not easily make connections between remote events and their own lives, unless these concern the emotions or self-interest. The wire services and news agencies are a steadying, *objectifying* influence upon this apparatus of conception, with their more stringent insistence upon factuality, but they too are ultimately feeding the same mechanism and are drawn into the same pattern of explanation. Like the explorers who preceded them, they are mapping the world on a principle of perpetual extension, starting with the known and adding some element of the previously unknown. The explorer always leaves one shore in order to reach another; he belongs to one place and travels in another. He brings—automatically—one civilization to scrutinize another. Reporting is exploration carried on by other means.

A kind of inevitability of domination is thus built into the Western conception of the world. The globe is seen in terms of the West's need for it. The following quotation comes from the opening page of a work about the exploration of South-East Asia written at the turn of the century:

The failure of the lands of south-eastern Asia to make a strong appeal to the imagination of the peoples of Europe is to be ascribed, however, not to their intrinsic unimportance, nor yet to any lack of wealth, of beauty, or charm, or of the interest that springs from a mysterious and mighty past. The reason is to be sought solely in the mere accident of their geographical position. Lying as they do midway upon the great sea-route which leads from India to China, it has been the fate of these countries to be overshadowed from the beginnings by the immensity and surpassing fascination of their mighty neighbours.[11]

Built into this statement is the 'ego' of an organizing, observing, ordering, rationalizing civilization. Every step taken towards enlightenment involves carrying the weight of all the past conceptions and misconceptions of the observing civilization. No explorer and no reporter work alone, for each brings with him that totality of past observing which has become part of his culture and therefore of his own conceptual apparatus. Every great journey of exploration began with an hypothesis, with an intention derived from need. Prince Henry the Navigator's journeys began as part of Portugal's policy of hot pursuit of the defeated Moors, followed by an attempt to secure some of the Indian trade which had been monopolized by the cities of Italy. The bees-wax, ostrich feathers, Negro slaves and gold which were brought back from successive journeys down the coast of West Africa established their own continuing market. The progress of European colonialism hung upon inquiry founded upon hypotheses as to what might be found and obtained. The tremendous worlds of Africa, Asia and South America (at first North America, too) were external worlds gradually 'domesticated' into the purview of the dominant societies.

It is just a century since the famous explorer-journalist H. M. Stanley stood before the Manchester Chamber of Commerce and declared:

> There are 50 millions of people beyond the gateway to the Congo, and the cotton spinners of Manchester are waiting to clothe them. Birmingham foundries are glowing with the red metal that will presently be made into ironwork for them and the trinkets that shall adorn those dusky bosoms, and the ministers of Christ are zealous to bring them, the poor benighted heathen, into the Christian fold.[12]

It has perhaps taken a hundred years for us to become conscious, as a civilization, of the meaning embedded in such a statement and to become deeply embarrassed by it. Stanley was summing up a *report*. He was a newsman. His professional integrity was unassailable. But his information was collected under the inspiration of a socially accepted doctrine of colonialism, in which the pursuit of loot, markets and the Christian faith were subsumed into a single quest, which was undoubtedly emotionally uplifting for his audience in imperial England.

Even at the time of Stanley the imperialist view of the world was an ancient one, with an earlier history which seemed as terrible to

Stanley's contemporaries as his view appears exploitative and disrespectful of indigenous cultures to us. When Vasco da Gama explored the coast of Africa he found a string of civilizations which were part of a complex international economy utterly unknown to the Portuguese, for whom it appeared to be a source of legitimate loot. Whole cities were seized without any protest on the part of their astonished inhabitants. Franciscan friars were the first ashore, carrying their tall crucifixes and singing Te Deums to the inhabitants while da Gama's men plundered their homes.[13] The sailors carried in their heads a legitimizing image of what it was they were doing, unshocked by what their eyes beheld: an image of Africa and the East and its peoples which had been accumulating through centuries as more and more of the world began to materialize before the amazed eyes of European explorers.

The more cynical of Third World intellectuals would point out the parallel between these early contacts between the civilizations of Europe and Africa and those journalistic ones of today. They might argue that the doctrine of free flow replaces Christianity as the West's 'cultural gift', and that while chanting hymns of freedom, democracy and development, the transnational companies turn newly independent African nations into branch-plant economies. The problem is one of inequality leading to injustice, a habit of imposing needs and attitudes upon societies where they do not fit and then assuming that the observed society is congenitally deficient rather than merely different. The very concepts of 'poverty' and 'development' are buried in this problem of crossed perceptions, in which the weaker, observed, objectified partner is made to accept the image held of it by the more powerful. Thus, all of the issues which arose from colonialism and imperialism are present in or are read into the contemporary argument over the alleged 'imbalance' in the flow of news, and the apparent ineradicable ethnic bias built into the reporting of the South by professional reporters from the North.

When a European or American reporter goes to Asia or Africa and discovers 'shortages', 'instability', 'corruption', 'crisis', he is often performing the same mental operation as Stanley; that is to say, he is *seeing* the society in the light of the prior images of his own society. A shortage of spare parts which prevents the Westerner from driving about is not necessarily an *abnormal* deficiency in a society which is used to having to walk for twenty miles. A different aspect of this process can be discerned in the famous agency reporter who always counts the Mercedes-Benzes at meetings of African political leaders as a *per se* sign of corruption; if, however, he were at a gathering called by the World Bank, the same reporter would probably not consider the numbers of Rolls-Royces or Mercedes a significant fact worthy of mention. The same conflicts of perception work in the reporting of politics. Any African country is vulnerable to a coup d'état committed by a small number of armed men; does this in itself constitute 'instability', or is it rather the common condition of governments which are attempting to construct new national entities out of territories which have been crudely carved from the geography of a defunct empire? When does a government become merely a 'regime', and by what criteria may it earn re-classification by Western journalists? What commodities have to be subject to scarcity—and in what geographical regions of a society—before they constitute a famine or economic dislocation? Scotch whisky? Chanel No. 5? Petrol? Bread? Rice? Bananas? The un-lamented former President of Uganda, Idi Amin Dada, used to attack the Western press for describing Uganda as 'almost bankrupt'; most of its people, he argued, lived on food which was directly provided by nature and were not affected in any way by trade balances, which were a 'bourgeois obsession' irrelevant to the conditions of Africa.

To be imprisoned inside the misinterpretation and misunderstanding of others can be a withering form of incarceration. It is a fate which can afflict whole nations and cultures as painfully as individuals. Today, two-thirds of the world's population is locked into a quickening spiral of deprivation, while committed avowedly to a goal known as 'development'. The new insistence on the part of Third World countries that some kind of restructuring must take place in the machinery of international communication is one part of their struggle to gain control of the processes of their economies. The sole achievement of many such societies hitherto has been political independence; the failure of the economic progress which was to have followed can be seen in terms of their own failure to follow through from independence to indigenous control of information. Economists and researchers thought, in the 1950s and 1960s, that imported radio, television, cinema and a foreign-owned press were all part of the process of modernization which consisted in the transference of capital goods and other industries. Today it is more widely held that the machinery of information, if it is controlled from outside, merely confirms the receiving country in a state of perhaps more hopeless dependence than before. Below the level of the president, the flag and the national anthem there is nothing to integrate the scores of cultures, ethnic and linguistic groupings, urban and rural populations if there is no indigenous information system. The war of words which UNESCO has focused upon is a concentrated expression of this newly felt need. Its ramifications for the West spread far and wide, for it will involve a complete re-drawing of the mental map of the world, a redrawing which was largely ignored when the old colonial empires crumbled in the 1950s.

II

Until the 1970s the poorer countries tended to accept the notion of 'development' in the terms in which the industrialized world used it. It was an historical milestone towards which all countries had painfully and progressively to evolve and which would end up with the whole of mankind living contentedly under democratically elected governments, with stable, well-nourished, prosperous, literate populations, respectful of the older nations' problems and ideals. Gradually, this concept began to seem a misleading, even damaging chimera, sold to the urbanized populations of the Third World by idealistic line-shooters, careless of destroying indigenous cultures and values.

Meanwhile, the media of the world offered the moral shocks of the Nigerian civil war, the brutal regime of Pol Pot in Cambodia, of the Ayatollah in Iran, Mrs Gandhi in India and Idi Amin in Uganda as evidence for a failure by Third World leadership. The lavish corona-tion of Emperor Bokassa, at the expense of the government of France, added a ghoulish absurdity to the collective image. The Third World was treated as irretrievably corrupt, a constant drag upon the economies of the West, a collection of aid-fed ingrates unworthy of the generosity heaped upon them. Birthrates stubbornly refused to fall, economies to grow, democratic systems to survive. A mood of cynical dismay swept through Western intelligentsia, reversing the naive idealism of the pre-Vietnam decades.

Certainly, the task of development had begun to look hopeless. Where the Third World's share of total world trade back in 1950 had been 32 per cent, it fell to 17 per cent by 1977. Its average per capita income was $180 a year, and only $100 in the poorest twenty-four countries at the UN—compared to $2,400 in the developed world. Projections of the future were uniformly gloomy: at best the average per capita income would improve by 1987 to $280, while that of the developed world would go up to around $3,400.[14]

In 1974, the UN proclaimed a New International Economic Order, a high-sounding term meaning merely that the Third World was now determined to reverse the spiral of increasing disparity between industrialized and non-industrialized sectors of the globe. Then they decided to go further and show how the *attitudes* of the West towards the problems of 75 per cent of the world's population were in themselves partly the cause of the latter's increasing deprivation. Exploitation had become structural in the culture of the West, and its 'disillusionment' and callous plundering were two sides of a coin. The Third World decided to turn the temperature high on the issue of cultural domination and news flow as a deliberate attempt to turn the terms of the debate over development against the West. The disillusionment of Western intellectuals and Western media with the Third World was now alleged to be the result of the same media's cumulative misrepresentation of the problems of undeveloped economies: the failure of 'development' became a universal assumption of the time. The Third World saw the mood, however, as cynical disregard dressed up as exasperated idealism.

The idea of a New International Information Order was born of this new démarche towards the media of the West. It involved taking the argument over development right into the hearths and homes of the industrialized world and confronting it with, in a sense, the failure of its own values, the illusions of its own superiority, the contrived irrelevance of its own notions of economic growth. 'The media have even conditioned public opinion in the developed countries to such an extent,' wrote Mustapha Masmoudi, Tunisia's Permanent Representative at UNESCO and former Information Minister, 'as to render it allergic to all claims and demands emanating from the Third World.'[15] One must wonder whether the analogy made between one 'order' (the economic) and the other (information) is not in itself a misleading trick of UN parlance, but none the less the challenge is a real one and the confrontation of values—moral, social, informational—might lead the Western media to fashion an information system more in line with the historical priorities of the world itself.

The roots of the idea of the new order lie deeper than the frustrations over the failure of Third World economies to catch up with those of the West; they lie in the very soil of the nineteenth century nationalist movements themselves. Mazzini spoke of 'the need to exist and have a name', and it has been the common problem of all nationalist movements, whether among European peoples or those of Africa, Asia and the Americas, to arouse their people to the new cultural imagery of nationhood, to force them to accept the inescapable destiny of the modern. It was one thing to make Piedmontese and Neapolitans in the last century realize that they were no longer merely Piedmontese and Neapolitans but quite another to give true meaning to the idea of being Italians, to create a new identity which would be spiritually and culturally reconciled with new forms of economic behaviour, new loyalties, new self-identities and citizenship. It has probably been even harder for Ashantis and Ibos to come to terms with being Ghanaian and Nigerian. The economic preachers of the West have partly neglected to realize that the will to prosper would probably be the result of rather than the cause of any new sense of citizenship.

Clifford Geertz has divided nationalism into four stages: the formation and crystallization of the movement, the triumph of the movement, the organization of statehood and the stage in which a new state is obliged to stabilize its relationship with other states and with the 'irregular societies' out of which the new states arose.[16] Of these, he argues that the first and fourth contain more far-reaching changes for every individual though these are far less spectacular in terms of external evidence than the second and third. The very start of nationalism necessitates grasping the cultural issue, confronting the myriad of racial, tribal, regional symbols and attitudes created by past eras and substituting for them a new phenomenon which is essentially abstract, artificial, self-conscious: a new political citizenship which changes all the notions held by every individual about who he is and what he is not. The problem is compounded by the presence in those countries, perhaps since the days of the first European colonizers, of a group who had come to see the world through the eyes of those colonizers and accepted their concept of progress, however much that may have entailed the abandonment of traditional values and cultures. 'The men who raised this challenge,' writes Geertz, 'the nationalist intellectuals, were thus launching a revolution as much cultural, even epistemological, as it was political. They were attempting to transform the symbolic framework through which people experienced social reality and thus, to the extent that life is what we make of it all, that reality itself.'

One might suggest today a fifth stage of nationalism, that in which, in order to gain some form of mental purchase on its problems, the nationalist elite passes through a period of revolutionary internationalism, in which a further abstraction is forced upon their societies. This is the specific ideological position of 'non-alignment', taken in consort with other nations towards all other ideological positions available in the world, in the hope of thus forcing others to accept and support the mental and cultural changes which lay behind the original act of nationalist self-assertion.

Both of the new 'orders', informational and economic, can be seen as expressions of this quest for *leverage* in creating new terms for internal social order, which in turn might make the concept of development into a viable reality. The use of the term 'order' also helps to create an international symbolism, a collective language of deprivation rationalized into goals, which can be realized only inside the context of international exchanges and institutions. At the moment of independence, the new governments felt that other more explicitly materialist matters should have priority. For the former imperial powers the information issue at the time of independence was a matter of domestic policy: the media of the new nations were left to function in a non-governmental, autonomous sphere. The Third World leadership is now trying to integrate the issue into other dominating issues and place it upon an international agenda, from which Third World politicians hope to obtain benefits. New technology, new uses of the magnetic spectrum, new political and financial resources of various kinds, can all hopefully be extracted from the international politicization of the information issue. By turning the partial failure of the cultural role of nationalism into an international late imperial grievance, it becomes a cashable asset.

As far back as 1972, the General Conference of UNESCO drew attention to the way in which the media of the richer section of the world were a means towards 'the domination of world public opinion or a source of moral and cultural pollution'. In 1973, in Algiers, there took place a meeting of heads of state of non-aligned countries, which attempted to rally all of the developing world to take concerted action in mass communications to promote a better interchange among themselves and release themselves from dependence upon the exports of the richer nations. The Algiers conference demanded the 'reorganization of existing communication channels which are the legacy of the colonial past and which have hampered free, direct and fast communications between them [the developing nations]'. The concepts which were established in international parlance at that conference have been powerful in subsequent years in that they supplied the labels for many of the topics in the present controversy in the period following the oil crisis of 1973–4 when the position of the developing world has become politically much stronger and more concerted in its confrontation with the West. These concepts were 'cultural alienation', 'imported civilization' and 're-personalization'. They meant that the unfettered flow of information and entertainment from the developed to the developing nations, maintained in the name of freedom of expression as practised in the former group of countries, was leading to a decline in the faith of developing nations in their own traditions and to a kind of spiritual vacuum which is fillable only by further importation of the offending material. Three years later, in 1976, the ministers of information of the same countries met in New Delhi and advanced the same arguments, perhaps rather more strongly. In the meantime, the argument had developed a fine head of steam and had become one of the principal items on the agenda of geo-political disagreement. It was at this point, moreover, that the developing nations' spokesmen adopted the wider aim of the New International Information Order, which was an attempt to sloganize in UNese a varied programme of urgent reforms in the field of information, which would provide the developing world with the material means to preserve their cultures, reverse the bias in the flow of information, restore the balance of political credibility between the sectors of the world and exploit information as a crucial tool in the task of economic development.

Finally, late in 1978, the UNESCO General Conference agreed its new Declaration on the Mass Media, which, although it was much 'softer' on the West than the latter had feared, gave even greater prominence to the tag phrase 'free and balanced flow', by which the developing nations mean to stress the desirability of reversing the imbalance without snatching away the freedom within which the imbalance arose in the first place. The declaration was inevitably going to become the basis for several rounds of international struggle which would be fought in future years over such varied matters as the right of Western journalists to continue writing as they wished about Third World societies and governments, the right of Britain, France and the US to continue exporting large quantities of their domestic entertainment material to other parts of the world and the sharing out of communication resources and technology.

There is a conflict between the needs of the Third World as they have been defined in these international gatherings and the media doctrines by which the information of the West is created and distributed. It is precisely within the orbit of the doctrine that the media industries of the West exercise their power—without the sense of right, without the ideological commitment to free flow, the Western nations (or those of them principally involved in international dissemination of entertainment and information) would be unable to pursue their traditional policies. The two positions are thus conceptually irreconcilable, although various makeshift interim deals have been contrived.

It is arguable that the setting up of the MacBride Commission was in itself intended to produce the intellectual compromise sought for by many involved in UNESCO. But the MacBride Report can merely take the controversy one stage further, after bequeathing some thousands of pages of fresh research and discussion material to those already yellowing on the shelves of UNESCO. For behind the argument over the New International Information Order lie the facts of history; what the issue really entails is coping with the long-term psychic consequences of colonialism and protecting the world against the intensification of the process of dependence in the late twentieth century, the era of advanced electronics and satellite-born information.

The most familiar summation of the demands for the New Order is that provided by Mustapha Masmoudi, the most noted fighter for the new cause among Third World statesmen. He has fought this case before UNESCO, by submission to the MacBride Commission, and by presentation at many international gatherings and conferences. The Declaration on the Mass Media agreed at the November 1978 meeting of UNESCO was the first tangible result of the pressure for a new order, although the protagonists achieved but a fraction of what they had hoped for.

The requirements as set out by Masmoudi consist partly in a scheme to 'eliminate the after-effects of the colonial era' in the collection, editing, selection and dissemination of news.[17] The developing countries must devise their own national communication policies which provide for the interchange of information at regional and local levels and the exchange of expertise, journalists and technicians among themselves, while working with developed countries to establish their media and train their personnel. Great stress is placed upon the need for a campaign to make the developed countries aware of the deficiencies in the present arrangements through conferences and seminars but also through curtailing the monopolies of the transnational agencies by procuring more equitable use of satellites and other networks. The developing world should also promote its own cultural improvement by constructing tax policies to help creative writers and artists and aid them in benefiting from the rewards of their labours. The new order also entails propagandizing the West to 'decolonize' its information resources, encourage them to pay more and better-informed attention to the Third World countries and their problems and to see that their reporters take care to check the accuracy of what they say and write; the pernicious activities of foreign radio stations are likewise to be curtailed, the output of national news agencies and newspools in the developing world is to be better respected, and the media of the developed world is to be encouraged to make use of it. The dislike long felt among developing nations towards the non-specialist 'special' correspondent who comes, like a visiting fireman, to report a developing nation's problems and then depart is given special attention. Such persons are to be encouraged to acquire appropriate comprehensive knowledge before they set out 'so as to be able to assess problems and concerns correctly and not see merely the sensational or anecdotal aspect of events, refrain from hasty judgements, free themselves of any distorting ideological lense through which they might be tempted to judge events and people, guard against all bias or prejudice and endeavour to ensure that their conclusions correspond to reality'.

A major programme of activities is also recommended for the international agencies, UNESCO in particular. The central aim is the training of Third World journalists and technicians and general promotion and support of the media in developing societies 'in a spirit of collective self-sufficiency'. Great emphasis is placed on international support for research into methods for transferring technology from North to South, and for promoting social change through communication. Among the demands is a plan for a new tax to be collected by all those developed economies which export cultural works, the proceeds of which would be used to create an international copyright fund administered by UNESCO. There is also considerable pressure for international organizations to help the new order's propaganda campaign. This in itself demonstrates a faith in the capacity of mass media to change people's minds, which is largely absent among the actual practitioners of the mass media.

Among the scores of pronouncements, demands and schemes,

there are a large number which ascribe new duties and responsibilities for governments and institutions and many which are designed to promote justice between nations and guarantee an abundant flow of the appropriate expertise to the regions in need of them. Alas, there are, however, few suggestions of ways in which the freedom of the journalist might be improved in any society. Rather the reverse. Masmoudi desires that measures are taken 'to ensure that journalists and writers show the utmost prudence and themselves verify the reliability and authenticity of all material, data, or arguments used by them which might tend to intensify the arms race'. He wants also 'to ensure that journalists respect the laws of the country and the cultural values of different peoples, and acknowledge that the right of peoples to make known their own concerns and to learn about those of other peoples is as important as respect for individuals'. Perhaps the most puzzling measure is his demand 'to put an end to the pernicious activities of foreign stations established outside national frontiers'. One searches in vain for any attempt to renew or regenerate the great movement for intellectual freedom which launched the national movements among colonial peoples in the last two generations. Where many of the founders of the new Third World nations—though admittedly not all—were demanding cultural and political liberty, Masmoudi's statement of the new order is a rather stuffy bureaucratic document, constructed partly to satisfy states which have abandoned personal liberty in favour of various kinds of regimentation.

Masmoudi draws attention moreover to 'new conceptions' of access to information which include the regulation of the right to information by preventing abusive uses of the right of access, and the definition of 'appropriate criteria to govern truly objective news selection'. Above all, it is in the area of the treatment of reporters themselves that the new order has become highly controversial, to say the least. Journalists everywhere are to be granted the right to professional self-regulation and effective machinery is demanded to protect them against undue or improper demands made by their employers; but such privileges are only provided in exchange for adherence to certain principles, which are to be enshrined in further international documents and enacted in the domestic legislation of all the states concerned. False or distorted information concerning individuals or communities is to be corrected publicly and the author concerned subjected to sanctions. 'No social group should have the prerogative of not being held accountable to the community to which it belongs.' The new order thus places great store by the right of a system of correction which ultimately would reside with the offended state concerned, which in turn would have a right to insist upon publication of communiqués rectifying and supplementing the false or incomplete information previously published. A new supranational organization would reinforce this new right which would call the guilty individual to account; it would consist of representatives of states and of the journalistic profession, together with 'neutral figures known for their moral integrity and competence in matters of information'.

Finally, the plans for the new order go into some detail on the equitable distribution of the electro-magnetic spectrum and the regulation of satellites. This is seen as one aspect of a new international right to communicate. Telecommunication tariffs are to be lowered, especially those which currently penalize low outputs, so that communication from developing to developed nations becomes cheaper. The plan also provides for the development of new techniques for stopping satellites spreading their signals beyond national boundaries and otherwise violating the cultural heritage of others by thrusting unwanted entertainment at their populations.

It is not hard to see why the media institutions of the developed world have hurried to condemn such plans, while at the same time offering various forms of international aid such as the free training of Third World journalists. This has not prevented the concept of the new order gaining ground and widening its acceptance, to the point where it has become an unavoidable item on the international agenda. For many in the Third World the proposals seem a useful platform from which to harangue the Western nations and make a number of other well-justified demands of them. For the West, almost every proposed measure entails an unacceptable intrusion of government into the sphere of information. For the managers and practitioners of the media it promises a long period of intense misery for the free press. The Soviet Union and its close allies can manage to digest the New International Information Order without great difficulty, although aspects of it are a little hard for certain communist countries to stomach. The developing nations have little to lose from it, except for those which have managed to acquire a non-governmental press.

Whatever threats the New International Information Order may hold for the 'free' press, there is no doubt that its cause is a just one. As we shall see, the imbalance which exists between North and South in the field of information is now deplorable and the gaps in *con-*

sciousness demonstrated in the journalism of the developed world undoubtedly help to foster the material inequalities. Within the wealthier nations—to which the developing nations are to a great extent financially locked—the doctrine of a free press and an open information system is culturally and politically crucial. The fact that it is also the sustaining doctrine of a series of important industries does not diminish its psychological and social importance.

For more than a century now this relatively small group of powerful nations has assumed that it enjoys a permanent flow of true and accurate information about the affairs of the world, as a result of the freedom under which its journalists and editors perform their professional tasks. Indeed, so deeply entrenched is this doctrine that the inhabitants of these countries have, for the most part, long accepted its universal applicability; they believe that the free unhindered flow of information and comment would benefit all societies at all times, not merely their own. It is thought to keep government responsible and free from corruption; it is thought to render decision-makers nationally accountable and lead to rational judgements in the administration and economy; it is thought to be a means for preventing power drifting into the hands of self-seekers and wrong-doers. The doctrine has become the prop and mainstay of a series of interconnected industries which purvey information (and entertainment) within and beyond the borders of the countries concerned: radio, television, the cinema and theatre, magazine and book publishing, news agencies and advertising companies—together with all the manufacturers of the equipment which supports these—benefit from the special protection possible in a society which manifests the belief that, whatever exceptions and limitations are imposed, there should be a free dissemination and collection of information. So ingrained is the doctrine that the Western countries cannot believe that their pursuit and development of this freedom can do anything but good for themselves and for all others.

The problem is simply that there is no room in the long run for conflicting information doctrines within a world which is becoming increasingly interconnected. The free flow of one section of the globe merely swamps the culture of others. The free interplay of giant corporations, earnestly desired by the liberals of one society as a way of rendering capitalism responsible, leads to the rest of the world becoming the great battlefield on which these transnational bodies compete with one another. Free flow enhances freedom only between equals and the imbalance brought about by this *kulturkampf* conducted in the international arena will only begin to recede when and if a significant section of the now developing nations themselves become financial and political world powers.

The proponents of the New International Information Order tend to underplay the complexities of the cultural problems of dependence. Many of them are economists or politicians who have paid little attention hitherto to the frivolities of cultural policy. They are part of the new élite of the developing world who themselves form the first or second generation of administrators and business people since national independence was achieved. They still feel some of the afterglow of the achievement of that independence. Until now, the fathers and mothers of independence in many African and Asian countries have been content to live on the culture of the metropolitan West, of Paris, London, Amsterdam, New York. In the major cities of the developing continents they are the watchers of Western imported television programmes, which only relate to the élite populations. Now they have discovered that independence must be taken a stage further into the cultural fold and pressure must be placed on the radio and television companies (which are normally state-owned) and on the newspapers (which are state-influenced and sometimes state-owned) to indigenize their output, to play down the imported entertainment material and emphasize local news, local and regional culture, indigenous entertainment. The demand entails a considerable conflict of interest, since it is, in most such countries, not the 'masses' but the elite which has had to sacrifice its preferred tastes. Whatever the outcome of its government's policies, that same elite will demand and will continue to enjoy that forbidden culture through overseas travel and imported records and cassettes. The information gap runs right through the developing nations as well as between North and South. The demand for a new order represents the attempt to re-guarantee a threatened political independence rather than a deeply felt desire to partake in the indigenous culture.

The problems of cultural dependence and domination are quite different in kind from the problems of industrial and economic status with which they of course overlap. The former reach deep into the psyche and pose problems of identity which a few poets and novelists of the Third World have chosen to make their main themes. Take, for example, the poem of Okot p'Bitek, the Ugandan exile, entitled 'The Song of Lawino', about a woman who perplexedly laments her husband's preference for a Westernized rival, and describes the strange world which he has entered:

And they dress up like white men,
As if they are in the white man's country.
At the height of the hot season
The progressive and civilized ones
Put on blanket suits
And woollen socks from Europe,
Long underpants
And woollen vests,
White shirts;
They wear dark glasses
And neckties from Europe.
Their waterlogged suits
Drip like the tears
Of the *kituba* tree
After a heavy storm.[18]

She cries that her man has become 'a stump' after reading the books of white men. 'Ocol has lost his head in the forest of books.' The husband's long reply, in a parallel poem, is a kind of ritual vow to root out all forms of 'superstition'; he has fought the struggle for independence, has taken his degree in economics at Makerere and has spent years in detention during the struggle. For him the traditional culture is a constricting primitivism:

We will rip off
The smelly goatskin skirts
From the women
And burn them,
Cut all the giraffe hair necklaces
And elephant hair bangles,
Break the ivory amulets
Cutting deep in the flesh
Of the upper arms,
Remove all the chains,
Ear-rings, nose-rings,
Lip-stops . . .[19]

Unfortunately, the proponents of the New International Information Order have virtually nothing to say about the emotional tensions and cultural contradictions presented by the new society to its intellectuals in their struggle for free and independent expression. They recognize that, at a certain level, an issue of identity exists for their societies, but they choose to speak only the language of geo-politics and bureaucracy. The very way in which the demand has become politicized reveals the rift between the politicians who advocate this new cause and their own writers and journalists. An East African editor said to this author:

> People forget that government held all of the power before in-dependence. It still holds all of the power. My fight for intellectual freedom is more important to me than the fight against Americani-zation. My task is to try to get the new system used to the idea that there could be *useful* but independent centres of opinion. But the Third World representatives at UNESCO are doing nothing but strengthening governments.

Living in the cultural shadow of the West multiplies and com-plicates the problems of the Third World journalist. It sets him to work in a peculiarly difficult and intractable field of forces. It is he who has to struggle with the aftermath of colonialism and endure the new constraints imposed by governments insecure about the loyalty of those around them. It is possible to feel very strongly the historical justice which lies behind the platform of the New International Information Order without greatly sympathizing with all its demands.

2. Cultural Dependence

Cultural dependence first became a talking point in the early days of the talkies. In the 1920s it was noticed that Hollywood products were responsible for four-fifths of all film screenings in the world. Hollywood had created the genre of the 'feature film', which started out as a staple entertainment form for the immigrant audiences of the United States. There was an enormous market for visual drama which played upon simple emotions and for which the ability to read English was not essential.

In Europe at that time film-makers were concentrating on presenting the classics and developing the cinema as a high art-form. Britain was among the countries most profoundly influenced by American films and it has never really succeeded in creating a viable indigenous film industry as a result of the way its market was seized by America over fifty years ago. Despite efforts by government to insist upon 'quotas' in cinemas and later in television, American films account today for 40 per cent of all films registered annually in Britain and in the feature film sector British production amounts to less than a quarter of the total number of films shown in Britain in an average year. In addition, American capital is heavily invested in the indigenous cinema of many European countries. Half of the budget of the Italian film trade association (ANICA) is held by Americans and anything up to 90 per cent of the cash invested, in some years, in British films has been American.

What happened in the film industry in the first decade or two of its existence was that a small number of American companies constructed a complex cartel around the genre of the feature film, stretching from the studio floor via the producers' offices to the business of distribution and exhibition in cinemas. If one imagines a similar phenomenon occurring in printed fiction it would mean that one company or one man was able to hire novelists straight from college, supply them with paper and typewriters and some standard plots and then publish the books on paper manufactured by the same company, ultimately selling the books exclusively in its own bookstores. In the cinema, the chain of control went in fact even further than this, for Hollywood created the 'star system', which was really a branch of the public-relations business; the star system enabled vast audiences to be captivated and milked of their time and dollars and established more firmly than would otherwise have been possible the linkages between production studios, exhibition houses and the minds of the audience. It meant that films could be made to strict, tried and trusted formulae, that studios could be turned into creative factories, guaranteeing continuous employment for those fortunate enough to be hired and that profits of breath-taking proportions could be generated.

For America, the film industry was, and is, legally a medium of expression, protected by the First Amendment to the Constitution, which guarantees freedom from prior restraint in all matters relating to information and opinion. The moguls of the movie industry largely policed themselves and ensured that nothing emerged from their factories which would offend or astonish or otherwise unduly attract the attention of the political world. For the investors, producers, writers and actors there was a free flow of movies throughout America's vast and eager market, but for those other cultures around the world which wished but could not develop their own secure cinema industry there began a period of almost complete dependence upon American products. There was no escape at all for those nations which are linked to the United States by the further bond of a common language.

It is not difficult to imagine the implications of the same processes of 'media imperialism' as it is practised in other entertainment branches of the communications network by Britain, France, America and other industrialized societies upon the emerging nations of the Third World. For here we have to reckon with not merely a single popular medium but with the whole range of print and electronic media which are of extreme importance to nations attempting to define their own political and cultural symbols and identity, whose media are, in very many instances, heavily subject to foreign nations' ownership. The free flow enjoyed by the donor society becomes an uncontrollable avalanche at the receiving end. According to figures published in 1974, for example, more than half of all the programmes shown on television in Chile, 34 per cent of those in Colombia, 62 per cent of those in Uruguay and 84 per cent in Guatemala were of American origin. American exports of feature films accounted for 50 per cent of all films shown in Chile in 1969, 50 per cent of all shown in Colombia, 58 per cent of those in Uruguay and 70 per cent in Bolivia, Brazil, Ecuador, Paraguay, Peru and Venezuela, to take a number of South American societies at random. Similar figures can be produced for virtually all of the emerging nations of Asia, Africa and the Middle East.[1] In Thailand, for example, which affords a case of massive dependence in many cultural fields, 90 per cent of all films shown to the public were American.

Since the mid-1970s, however, many of these countries have started to pursue a policy of indigenization, with varying effect. There are several countries within the developing world which are today considerable exporters of entertainment material—Mexico, India and Hong Kong are prominent among them. There have also been several attempts to pool news material from developing countries into regional or international non-aligned agencies and even to start a new multi-national news agency, but it is too soon yet to see whether these are ever going to challenge the present dominance of the Western news agencies. What many fear is that existing relationships in the field of politics and economics between the various sectors of the world will be perpetuated by cultural exports, and that entertainment material will continue to create an awareness of American culture which contributes to the receiving society's continued economic dependence upon the goods and life-styles of the major donor society. In other words, the flow of media exports acts as a kind of ideological prerequisite for the flow of other material exports.

Of course, the mere existence of a quantity of material is of little avail if it is not intrinsically admired, or trusted or needed. The Soviet Union is a great exporter of films but these do not appear in themselves to have captured the attention of many millions of peasants or urban dwellers in Third World countries. The Soviet Union is also among the very largest of international broadcasters, putting out about 2,000 hours of radio programmes every week in eighty-four languages; but Soviet Radio, according to studies carried out in Africa, seldom reaches more than one or two percentage points of listeners, while the BBC, with far fewer hours broadcast, reaches more than 50 per cent of listeners at any given moment in eastern, central or western Africa. This is in part a case of post-imperial hangover, but capitalist media products in general are far more powerful than communist ones in the countries of the developing world—even in countries where political and military links exist with Eastern Bloc countries.

American influence has been steadily growing in almost all fields of information, though the present phase of American overseas cultural policy is not very old. For much of the present century American industry was content to leave British and French media interests to hold the centre of the world stage. The major networks of the world, especially those which linked Asia, Africa and Europe, were largely British, while France held sway in large parts of South America and the East. The communications networks—in transport, telephone, telegraph, broadcasting and the press—grew out of the imperial routes which passed through London and Paris. An economic network lay behind the system of imperial preferences of Britain and that in turn was expressed in and was aided by the communication linkages. Even today the telephone and telegraph links between India and Europe and Africa and Europe reveal the colonial control systems of the past. It is still sometimes easier to telephone or to travel from one part of Africa to another by way of London rather than direct. Reuters and Havas controlled the flow of news around the world and the two American agencies, AP and UPI, accepted something of a back seat until the years immediately prior to the war, when they insisted on their own direct news exchanges with Japan and other nations.

America eventually broke the tight hold of Reuters in the late 1940s, in the interest of creating a more balanced flow of news into America, one not mediated by an organization which, although not controlled by the British government, appeared to impose a British set of priorities and values on the news of the entire globe. America mounted an offensive against the British communications network in its control of the oceanic cables as well as the software of news and information. The Executive Manager of AP, Kent Cooper, published a book in 1942 which attacked the European news cartels and the 'tenacious hold that a nineteenth century territorial allotment for news dissemination had upon the world'.[2] A major campaign was mounted in the 1940s in Congress (with the help of Senator Benton, former Assistant Secretary of State and later President of *Encyclopaedia Britannica*[3]) to break down the barriers which prevented the worldwide expansion of American media enterprises—in books, cinemas, magazines, news. Freedom of the press was deliberately made a branch and tenet of US foreign policy. The media enterprises themselves worked to rally public opinion on the issue, a factor which became all the more important in the course of the early stages of the Cold War, when the cause of free information aroused the imagination of the West in the struggle against the totalitarian world.

In nations which had done away with private capital altogether the cause of a free press was both political anathema and popular dynamite; the Soviet Union's leaders both hated and feared it. American newspaper publishers and newspaper editors passed resolution after resolution at their annual conventions emphasizing the crucial role of free information in the openness of American society. It was in the context of the Cold War fervour that AP and UPI planned their massive expansion into all the news centres of the world. America thus energized her information economy in a mood of ideological stridency, in which she felt herself to be both victim and saviour.

Advertising, so overwhelmingly dominated by the US, is an important historical factor of the West's version of a free press. Until well into the nineteenth century most of the European and American press was subject to various forms of political and governmental patronage; not until the present century was it possible, in many parts of Europe, for newspapers to operate under a banner of political neutrality. It was advertising that enabled the doctrine of impartiality or objectivity to take root in newspapers. These are, of course, only relative terms—the objectivity achieved was in relation to the prevailing political and economic forces in the nations concerned.

But advertising has not been able to play a similar role in the evolution of Third World media. Advertising has been unable to manifest itself as a source of *independent* patronage of indigenous media because of American dominance in the advertising industry. The twelve largest advertising agencies of the United States are exactly the same companies which form the top twelve advertising agencies in the world. Even in West Germany, France, Britain, Australia and Canada, half of the major agencies are American and in a large number of countries in Europe, Asia and South America, the largest agency in the land is a branch of one of the American majors. Canadian radio and television are wholly dependent upon advertising placed by American agencies.

Of course, the total advertising expenditure in the developing world is but a fraction of the total world advertising market. In 1972, among the twelve states with the largest annual advertising expenditure, only one, Brazil, was a developing nation. Its $560 million worth compares with $23,130 million gross in the US itself, with $1,734 million in Britain and $1,660 million in France. However, Brazil's advertising was higher than that of Italy and the Netherlands and many other European countries. Meanwhile, India, with its vast population, had acquired an advertising market of only $93 million, Iran only $34 million, Egypt $32 million, Morocco $6·6 million and pre-oil crisis Saudi Arabia less than $5 million. Sixty-one per cent of the total advertising market of the world lay in North America and a quarter in Europe. Asia, Latin America, Africa and the Middle East, between them, mustered only 13 per cent of the world's market. The American domination of even such relatively small markets is disproportionately high. McCann-Erickson, for example, placed $6 million worth of business in India in 1975 and Ogilvy, Benson and Mather a further $4·5 million. Three-quarters of all advertising in India comes from the Indian government, leaving the private sector with perhaps $25 million in all. For the US agencies the benefits of this particular form of 'free flow' are easy to see: the total sum earned in all countries outside the US by the ten largest US agencies in 1975 was slightly less than the total earned by the same companies inside the US: $2,794 million compared to $2,946 million. These companies have come to depend very greatly upon the export of their expertise, even to the Third World, though it represents only a fragment of the total. Their role outside the United States is of relatively recent growth—in 1960 this part of their business was about a fifth of what it was by the mid-1970s.[4]

The mere recital of figures does little to illustrate the true implications of media dependence. The presence of overseas owners of indigenous newspapers, the flow of advertising controlled by foreign agencies, the dependence upon foreign equipment to supply the whole of a radio or television system and the importation of foreign mass entertainment material in cities which have sprung up only in the post-colonial era all mean that the whole outlook of a nation's media—including the training of its writers, producers, salesmen, actors, cameramen—takes place in the context of a foreign culture. It is easy to talk loftily about 'exposure to foreign values', but on the ground it means that local journalists are trained to edit agency wire copy as if they were preparing material for a foreign public; announcers are trained to behave as if they were addressing audiences of English or French or German; programme formats are taken off the shelf from the US or British or French networks. Whatever indigenous elements are introduced, are found battling against what is at root a foreign medium, with foreign values. In television (which is an important medium in South America, though not in Asia or Africa), the distortion is made even worse by the use of American material, which may in any case represent a high proportion of total material, in the hours of greatest viewing, thereby multiplying its impact. Where governments have attempted to force back the tide of imports there has, in some cases, been almost no expertise on which to build. The whole organization of the medium has been that of a receiving country, its management and production skills being those of arrangers of foreign material. Television is for them a medium which arrives in cans. It is particularly grievous in countries like Thailand, which has an enormously rich visual culture of its own, to find that none or almost none of the traditional store of symbols and imagery of the society passes into the new medium.

In no sense is the one-way flow of media products a mere accident, a peripheral bonus added to the business activity of the exporting firms and nations. There are clear signs that media exports have become necessary to the exporting industries concerned. We have already seen a good example of this in advertising. In the field of television programmes a similar pattern is emerging. Britain, the largest exporter of television after the US, is a country whose public broadcasting service, the BBC, has become subject to considerable financial pressure. It has been difficult for Britain to maintain its high standards of programming on the basis of its domestic market. The licence fee is insufficient to pay the enormous staff required by the BBC to maintain a constant flow of home-made material in two television channels. The commercial television companies of Britain have also felt the need to diversify, since their very high profits cannot be guaranteed indefinitely—each company's franchise is subject to periodic withdrawal and reapplication. Profits may not be invested at will, since a public authority supervises all the peripheral activities of the companies licensed to make programmes. In the late 1970s exportation of programmes has multiplied, the BBC's earnings from overseas quadrupling between the mid-1960s and mid-1970s. All television has a place for high-quality foreign products but developing nations can easily become addicted to them, their audience mesmerized by skilfully made and perhaps only partly comprehended documentaries, series and serials. French television has also made great inroads into the television markets of its own former colonies and other developing nations. No other nation, including Britain, has succeeded in benefiting from the great economies of scale afforded by the vastness in size and wealth of the American domestic television market. It is impossible for foreigners to compete in that market against the present incumbents, apart from the special case of the American public broadcasting system, whose hundreds of stations have created an important market for certain kinds of European product. No developing nation could hope to reverse the flow of information in the television field—entry into either the American or the European market would require an investment far beyond the capacity of any such society.

The major countries of the West have experienced for well over a century now the conditioning processes which turn variegated societies into homogeneous audiences and into markets ready for media and advertisers to exploit. Since the middle of the nineteenth century the industrialized nations have removed the barriers of illiteracy which once kept the majority of the population structurally immune to the influence of print; they have readjusted the population share between urban and rural, between élite and non-élite; where a single society was divided into many linguistic groups single languages have come to dominate across large stretches of terrain while other languages have acquired subsidiary or peripheral status; even tribal survivals have been to a great extent abolished and their vestiges coaxed and cajoled into a single organized market system and a single political structure.

In the developing world, the lines of literacy, tribalism, linguistic and caste loyalty, urban and rural, élite and non-élite, continue to divide societies into groups of people with widely divergent attitudes and different levels of commitment to and understanding of the modern state. The entire range of Western theories of the media are predicated upon a single mass market, an ethnographic impossibility in the context of developing societies. The distribution of media products, print and non-print, simply cannot be conducted with the automatic ease of Western societies; geography, transport, human and physical structures do not exist with which to send material out into the audience. Indeed, in a sense, the 'audience' has not yet been fully created. It is also uncertain whether this audience will evolve along the same lines as those of the developed countries.

Where developed countries have made significant attempts to create indigenous media, but in the Western manner, they have been vexed with competition from the West, either in the form of rival media products or competitive investment in the local media itself. Asia alone has over 140 English-language daily newspapers circulating among the new élite of the cities, who would otherwise be the core audience for indigenous media; many of these papers are now, of course, locally owned but most are not and they act as a lure for the advertising revenue and circulation revenue of sizeable audiences, in some cases the whole of the potential target public of advertisers in those countries. These newspapers have fewer distribution problems than their vernacular competitors since the audience of the former are usually concentrated in the cities. It is also cheaper to produce the English-language papers because they can more easily benefit from more modern printing technology; in any case, it takes far less newsprint to reproduce the same information in English as in most of the Asian writing systems (apart from Chinese), the languages of India, for example, requiring twice as much expenditure on newsprint for the same material. As fast as an audience attractive to advertisers develops in Asia, it is mopped up by non-vernacular media, with the profits often accruing to one of the great Western newspaper magnates.

Outside Japan, Asian newspaper circulations are minute, hardly averaging above 6 copies per 100 inhabitants in most countries of the continent.[5] Where no less than $23 worth of advertising backs every copy printed of the average newspaper in Japan,[6] the Indian newspaper manages to collect $9, most of it placed by the government's own advertising bureau. It is little wonder that the average Asian must work for three weeks to earn the money for a year's subscription while in the West and Japan his counterpart would earn the money in two and a half days. The industrialized countries taken as a whole distribute 31 newspapers per 100 and the developing world only 2·9, ranging from 1·4 in Africa at the lowest to 7 in Latin America. Perhaps it is only fair to point out that newspaper circulation in Africa doubled over the decade to 1975 and increased by a fifth in Asia and a third in Latin America;[7] in North America and Europe, the newspaper has remained on the whole a stagnant medium in terms of audience spread. The advances made in the newspaper medium in the Third World have been made against overwhelming odds: newsprint is manufactured in very small quantities in the developing countries of Asia and Africa and the price of imported newsprint escalated painfully in the 1970s; the cost of distribution in the transportation-starved countries of the developing world have leaped upwards in similar proportion since the oil crisis of 1973; and the relative difficulty for an Asian publisher and editor to compete with Western products hungry for additional markets has increased rather than diminished over the years. The indigenous press thus suffers from a powerful conspiracy of circumstances which forces it to pit itself against the giants of the West.

To the outside observer, radio appears to be the easiest medium for a developing country to master. Its 'circulation' does not depend upon the spread of literacy, nor of physical transportation, nor of the growth of well-heeled consumers, nor necessarily upon advertising. It can use the vernacular languages, it can disregard physical distance, it is not to any important extent vulnerable to competing sources in the West. Where newspapers in Africa and Asia have been obliged to use out-of-date equipment until it falls apart, radio companies have been equipped only in recent times and should be able to function cheaply and efficiently. Moreover, problems of governmental versus private control should not prove a difficulty in practice, since governments have to set up broadcasting utilities in the first instance and do not have to go through the complex task of nationalizing, bribing, terrorizing editors to do their bidding. All of this is indeed the case and research studies indicate that most Africans, for example, have acquired their basic political knowledge of the world through listening to radio.

However, radio signals are not nearly as plentiful or as accessible in practice as it would seem. Africa and Europe are part of the same region in terms of spectrum planning at the International Telecommunication Union and both continents are obliged to reuse the same sections of the medium- and short-wave bands. There was a time when this presented no problems, but modern transmitters in Europe have grown more powerful and more numerous, causing havoc at times to African stations. Compared with the allocations of these bands made in the past to European countries, the African nations suffer from spectrum starvation. The average African transmitter spreads its signals out over 100,000 square miles—in Sudan each transmitter has a million to cope with. This compares with a figure of 1,600 square miles for the average American transmitter. It means that African radio engineers need to know their business very well indeed if their listeners are to get a reasonable service. But the information is not even available for them to do their job. The work of mapping the propagation of waves across much of the African continent and of studying ground-conductivity zone by zone has never been done, at least not on the scale of Europe and America, so that African radio stations are operating with inadequate spectrum allocation, insufficient transmission points, and in an absence of relevant data. Yet there are twenty African countries which at the beginning of the 1970s only possessed a single transmitter apiece. None the less, as Table 1 shows, use of radio has been growing fast.

Table 1: Growth of Radio Ownership 1960–76

ESTIMATED NUMBER OF RADIO RECEIVERS IN USE

Continent	Year	Total number (million)	Continent	Year	Total number (million)
Africa	*circa* 1960	4	Asia	*circa* 1960	22
	1970	16		1970	58
	1976	30		1976	113
Northern America	*circa* 1960	184	Europe	*circa* 1960	136
	1970	326		1970	233
	1976	454		1976	284
Latin America	*circa* 1960	14	Oceania	*circa* 1960	3
	1970	31		1970	8
	1976	58		1976	14

Source: UNESCO Statistics on radio and television 1960–76, Office of Statistics, Publication No. 23.

It is widely stated that the entire population of the world now lives within transmitting distance of a radio signal, and in theory this is so. The total number of radio receivers in the world passed the billion mark in about 1975. In Africa the number had more than doubled in a decade to around 28 million, in Asia to 108 million, in Latin America to 58 million. The developing world had acquired 160 million sets, compared to the developed world's 758 million. In terms of the spread of listening, the figures demonstrate even greater inequalities. There are 8 sets for every 100 inhabitants of the Third World and nearly 70 per 100 in the developed. Worse still is the fact that maintenance is more difficult in the developing continents and the statistics do not measure the number of sets which are not in working order at any given moment. The only area of the developing world with a major success story in radio is Latin America, which has already reached 24 sets per 100. Argentina now has nearly 40 sets per 100, which is higher than Western Europe. But there are countries in Asia where only 1 set exists for every 100 people (e.g., Afghanistan). In India the average is 2·5.

In television the position is, as might be expected, much more unequal between the two halves of the world, and many people argue that developing societies would do well to stay out of the television business altogether, since it opens up a great vista of endless and increasing dependence on Western programme exports. In Africa and Asia there are only a handful of countries which manage to reach 90 per cent of their population with a TV signal; half the countries concerned reached less than half of their populations. Argentina and Brazil and Uruguay are exceptions in the developing world; with their wealthy television industries they reach a large proportion of the population—more than 15 receivers per 100 inhabitants, compared with 31 for West Germany, 36 for Britain and 29 for the Soviet Union.[8] Many of the Middle Eastern nations, of course, are now very amply provided for with regard to receivers.

The culturally and politically debilitating effects of media dependence are perhaps most eloquently illustrated by taking an example not from the non-aligned or developing countries but from within the developed world itself. Canada has always been obliged to struggle to maintain a thriving indigenous culture because of the proximity of the United States with its enormous output of information and entertainment. To all intents Canada has been treated as part of a large North American market for films, television programmes and other media products. Its attempts to free itself from the gush of American exports have been ingenious, fitful and enterprising, but have never amounted to the imposition of quotas and tariffs. It has conceded the right of free flow and has suffered the consequences. One third of the $200 million a year spent at cinema box offices, for example, goes straight back across the border to the US distributors. Canada's efforts to establish a national cinema of its own have had—since the 1930s—to be conducted amid this constant drain of its resources.

In the 1940s, Canada was experiencing a period of particularly acute trade deficits with the United States and a fierce debate took place over the possibility of imposing a quota on American feature films. The Motion Picture Association of America finally convinced the Canadian government that what it needed was more frequent allusion to Canada in American movies, presumably to encourage more tourism north of the border and by this means a reversal of the payments flow. It is hard today to believe that Canada allowed itself to be thus fobbed off, but it is a matter of historical fact that a representative of Canada was specially appointed to reside in Hollywood and supervise small changes of dialogue and location in American films: escaping convicts would trudge their way to Canada rather than Oregon, lovers would elope to Ottawa rather than Chicago, stars would spend glamorous weekends in the Canadian Rockies.

In 1939, John Grierson had founded the National Film Board of Canada, supported with government funds. At first it produced a series of war propaganda films and then went on to create a major documentary school; at one point it tried to move into the field of feature films but was stopped after US interests raised objections with the Canadian government. Then after the war an anti-trust case was brought against the film industry within the United States which resulted in the film production companies being obliged to divest themselves of their ownership of cinema chains, on the grounds that these linkages resulted in a restraint of trade. Canada, however, lies outside the jurisdiction of American courts and the ownership of its cinemas was allowed to remain in the hands of the American majors; today, control of three-quarters of all Canadian cinemas lies with Paramount, which in turn is owned by Gulf and Western. Canadian independent film-makers have little access to exhibition in their own country. Canadian television flourishes but it purchases its vast stock of films for rerun from the same major film distributors as American television networks and therefore tends to go for the films which have already proved themselves to be popular with the cinema public.

Where Canadian film culture has fallen at the first hurdle it now stumbles at the second. Since the late 1960s there has existed a Canadian Film Development Corporation which tries to raise investment capital (like Britain's National Film Finance Corporation) to pay for Canadian production. The criteria for being considered appropriate for such help contain, as they should, the presentation of proof that the film will receive distribution and that the distribution contract will cover at least half of the budget; however, all of Canada's cinema chains are American-owned and the CFDC has developed very slowly indeed. The Canadian government, in a further bid to create an indigenous feature film industry, has signed a number of co-production treaties with European countries and is offering 100 per cent write-off against income tax to all investors in features. It is extremely difficult for a society to practise free flow of media and enjoy a national culture at the same time—unless it happens to be the United States of America.[9]

The paradox of Canada's dependence is that her use of modern telecommunication links of all kinds is greater than that of any nation on earth. She has used domestic satellites to bring television and telephone services to her scattered population since 1973 and half of her population was cabled by 1978. In the advanced field of informatics she has developed a domestic text service called Telidon, which promises to be the most sophisticated of all devices currently being pioneered in this area. Despite the technical headstarts which Canada constantly provides for herself, she has found that most of the equipment has to be imported and most of the content of her media consists of American material. Many Canadians treat the phenomenon today as a kind of running national crisis. No country in the world probably is more completely committed to the practice of free flow in its culture and no country is more completely its victim.[10]

Canada's basic problem is geographical. More than half of her population lives within 100 miles of the US border (i.e., within television signal distance) and 80 per cent live within 200 miles. The internal tension between French-speaking Quebec and the rest of Canada has led to a constant controversy over the respective legal powers of federal and provincial governments over communication questions and the result has been that a tidal wave of American culture has swept over the entire country. The constant increase in the flow of American capital into Canadian industry has turned Canada into a branch-plant economy and the cultural consequence is the growth of a branch-plant mentality. Canadian schoolchildren seem to know more about the American Constitution than the Canadian, more about US history than Canadian. American political trends are adopted in Canada as if by a law of nature—for example, the current mood favouring 'de-regulation' in the field of tele-communications which started up during the early months of the Carter administration has fed itself into Canada, where regulatory requirements are probably rather different from those of her larger neighbour. Where Pay-TV, satellite, cable networks and completely 'free' radio frequencies may be the best next stage in the US, the maintenance of national controls on new developments might be better for Canada, but the doctrines and ideologies which develop south of the border spread relentlessly, to the detriment of Canada's own self-management.

Just before the Second World War, Canada developed a national broadcasting system, CBC, modelled on Britain's BBC. Commercial stations were also permitted both in radio and television, and these have gradually grown in number, transmitting a large quantity of American programming in addition to the American signals which most of the population were already able to receive. In the 1970s, local cable stations have arrived and these transmit more material, mainly American. CBC, in order to hold on to a reasonable share of the audience, found it necessary to acquire the same popular American series, although in recent years it has attempted to build up its Canadian content above the 80 per cent level. Public service broadcasting has thus had to struggle in Canada against the forces of virtually untrammelled commercial television, something that the BBC and its counterparts around Europe have never had to face. The CBC's income comes direct from Parliament rather than via a viewers' licence fee, and she has had to find arguments for maintaining a high level of income both against those who complain that her share of the audience is too low (sometimes down to about 10 per cent) and against those who complain about the high level of American imported material used on CBC (acquired in order to raise the share of the audience). Confused public policies towards Canadian content in public broadcasting (inevitable in a country subjected to the ideological barrage of American private commercial television) have evolved alongside fierce commercialism. What compounds the problem of American competition for Canada, and all other societies subject to media dependence, is that the American import has already been paid for in its domestic market and its producers are merely trying to get a little additional jam from the Canadian market. The reverse is not true for a Canadian producer attempting to make a programme attractive to American audiences; in making his programme competitive on the international market, he would have to spend far more than his domestic market can provide.

The tragic paradox of Canada's technological advances is that they consist of ingenious devices (satellites, microwave, cables, etc.) for reaching the distant communities of Canada—English, French, Eskimo—who have hitherto been preserved from the American onslaught. Canada has now constructed a telecommunications system of great sophistication which will enable all Canadians, however distant from the US frontier, to be subjected to the same flow as the rest of the country. Canada's own Anik satellite may soon be sending out four complete American television network signals throughout its entire territory, while adding a few Canadian signals for the remoter areas which cannot yet receive them, and a number of Pay-TV channels carrying a mixture of Canadian and American material.

The same patterns of dependence are already appearing in the field of data processing. Canadian mining, insurance, oil, gas, credit and other companies store their data across the border in the US rather than creating their own national databases. Where a vast and wealthy market can create cheap and convenient facilities it can attract overseas custom very easily. Canada could create a viable market of its own but only on the basis of a considerable amount of national and governmental direction, which runs counter to the doctrine of free flow. None the less, there is great political pressure in Canada today for legislation which would prevent data being stored or processed in computers outside Canadian territory. The same dilemma—either free flow—or state intervention—seems to be affecting all the new communications systems. At the International Institute of Communications' 1979 annual convention in London, M. Alphonse Ouimet of Telesat, Canada put forward a plan for treating cable as a public utility monopoly which would be subject to the same kind of national controls as scarce over-the-air signals for conventional radio and television. A public authority could then regulate the content, ensuring that American material was balanced with indigenous and other foreign programmes. It would end the anomaly whereby a television station wishing to use foreign material has to purchase the right to transmit it programme by programme, while a cable operator merely snatches the entire content of a foreign signal out of the air and transmits it in its entirety to the client viewers. Cable stations acquire their television content for nothing and the proposed legislation, which would remove all such rights from the cable operators, would attempt to rationalize the methods of regulation and at the same time release Canada from its state of extreme dependence. The practicality of the plan is not wholly relevant here; nor is its political viability in a country in which cable operators have a powerful lobby in favour of the free-for-all status quo. What is important is the underlying realization in the plan that the escape of culturally dependent nations can only be through the imposition of national controls on imported material and services.

Canada is not, of course, a developing society in the normal sense of that overworked term. Its problem has been dealt with here because it has a very long experience of cultural dependence and because its history indicates that dependence is far harder to escape from than colonialism; it grows with the sophistication of technology and administration and it demonstrates the way in which the liberal doctrines of a dominant society are not necessarily liberal in their impact upon a dominated society. Each attempt to escape from the paradox, so to speak, at one end leads the victim into a further convolution of the underlying problems.

The new technologies are multiplying the dangers of cultural domination as well as the number of territories subject to it. As Leonard Marks, former director of the US Information Agency, put it:

> ... global electronic networks ... will pose realistic questions about information flow and cultural integrity. ... These networks will move massive amounts of information through high-speed circuits across national boundaries. Moreover, they will be effectively beyond the reach of the traditional forms of censorship and control. The only way to 'censor' an electronic network moving ... 648 million bits per second is literally to pull the plug. The international extension of electronic mail transmission, data-packet networks and information-bank retrieval systems in future years will have considerably more effect on national cultures than any direct broadcast systems.[11]

Leonard Marks was signalling the dangers inherent in the new technologies in order to help America avoid the political perils. But this very problem had already arrived on the agenda of international politics in the early 1970s at the instigation of President Kekkonen of Finland. In May 1973, Kekkonen launched forth on the topic in a speech which became a founding text in the movement towards a New International Information Order. He reminded his audience that the Declaration of Human Rights which was signed after the Second World War expressed the ideas of Adam Smith and John Stuart Mill—it was a restatement of *laissez-faire* ideas, an assertion of individual freedoms. 'But the freedom of the strong led to success and the weak went under in spite of this so-called liberty.' He presented a case which has gained rapid acceptance among the ninety new nations which have come into existence since the end of the war, as well as the acceptance of the communist countries. It will take far longer however, for his ideas to be accepted by a sub-stantial number of individuals and societies in the developed nations of the West.

In his speech, Kekkonen went on to say: 'Globally, the flow of information between states—not least the material pumped out by television—is to a very great extent a one-way unbalanced traffic, and in no way possesses the depth and range which the principles of freedom of speech require.'[12] Until the 1970s, it had not become evident that the information flow around the world was beginning to constitute a cause very similar to the great movement within European states in favour of press freedom in the late eighteenth and nineteenth centuries. After the Second World War it seemed to most people that the mere granting of political independence to new waves of nationalist leaders throughout Asia and Africa would automatically lead to the development of a general acceptance of the ideal of press freedom. To some it even seemed possible that China and the Soviet Union would gradually stabilize their systems to the point at which such freedoms would seem natural. It did not occur to many people until the last decade or so that information lay at the root of sovereignty and that the movement for independence would have to continue beyond the political stage into economic and informational struggles of equal intensity to those which had led to the first stages of the post-colonial era. The American defeat in Vietnam has perhaps done more than any other single event to change the world's image of the cultural power of America and its acceptance of it as necessarily a dominant force in the culture of the new nations. The defeat on the other hand has perhaps made America feel that its 'information presence' is all the more vital to it in validating its hold on global leadership, and this in turn has made the receiving nations all the more defensive.

The physical equipment through which the new electronic culture of the world is received by publics and audiences is subject naturally to the management of the same transnational companies which determine the parameters of the Western economy today. More and more of the software is also drawn into their compass or control and for this to circulate, homogeneous markets have to be created—audiences trained, as it were, to want what is on offer. The electronic culture rides roughshod over the subtle divisions and groupings of which traditional cultures consisted—indeed on which they depended. Perhaps the greatest single homogenizing force is the English language itself. (It is worth noting that the attack on the use of English is the main thrust of the campaigns of Quebec, Welsh, Irish, Inouit and many other peoples in attempts to preserve their cultural integrity). The dominance of English enforces a kind of one-way flow, even if both sides are communicating. This remains true even in cases where the native language is used. *Reader's Digest* and *Time* magazine, to take two examples, offer foreign language or overseas regionalized versions to their foreign readers, but they remain essentially American products and all who are influenced by them are drawn powerfully into the centre core of American values. These popular publications spread values more effectively than they spread information; they are emanations of the American spirit and are more powerful Americanizers than hamburgers or motor-cars or Coca-cola.

In its earliest days, even UNESCO itself inadvertently contributed to the idea that information dependence on the West was the route through which a society travelled towards the goal of independence. It created a number of 'minimum standards' for communication development. Every country was to strive to provide 10 newspapers, 5 radio receivers, and 2 cinema seats for every 100 of its population.[13] These were the 'thresholds' of development; by means of these devices, distributed in adequate quantity, a society would acquire new skills and attitudes and traditional society would start to slough off its reluctance to enter fully into the twentieth century. Inevitably, this attitude to modernization broke down, and the collapse of the Shah's regime in Iran was perhaps the most spectacular example of its rejection. There an indigenous traditional information system, Shi'ite Islam, discovered itself intact at the end of a decade or more of vigorous importation of Western culture and on the crest of a wave of oil prosperity. The whole quest for modernization was rejected along with the Shah and the electronic culture, technically advanced though it was, was suddenly seen to have been an excrescence, an imposition, a conflict-bearing overseas culture which appealed to a particular Westward-leaning élite, but which had not and could not penetrate the entire culture.[14]

Standing with the reporter in the same tradition as the medieval explorer is the modern tourist, gaping at the world through the same ethnocentric blinkers. Geographical mobility, which has spread throughout the nations of the developed world, carries with it a certain repertoire of expectations, contains its own implied perspective on the world as a whole, particularly towards the visited nations. Tourism has become a source of considerable profit to the large organizations which are concerned with exploiting the new mobility of the middle- and lower-middle-classes of the West and, like other aspects of the outwardly free-flowing culture of the West, creates a small but economically powerful specialist caste within the receiving country. One observer of the impact of tourism on the Caribbean has written:

Tourism rests on the active collaboration of West Indian élites with metropolitan agencies. National leaders have not only been incapable of reversing the tourist tide but, in many cases, have been its principal promoters and beneficiaries. Land-owning groups have benefited enormously from rising land values. Commercial and financial sectors linked to the import aspects of tourism participate profitably in the travel industry. . . . With the support of metropolitan agencies, West Indian leaders, in the epoch of decolonization and national liberation struggles, have led their societies into the sixteenth century.[15]

Tourism places the whole of the visited culture on sale, distorting its imagery and symbolism, turning its emotions loose, transforming a way of life into an industry. The real-estate market is heavily distorted, to the point at which indigenous peoples are deprived of access to their own land. A culture, in the worst instances, is turned from subject to object, from independent to dependent, from audience-in-its-own right to spectacle. The tool employed by the 'donor' nation to perform this task is the willing and active co-operation of local élites. It is not surprising that those in charge of the information companies of the West are perplexed to the point of anger when their right to perform the role of shaping the new cultural consciousness of the receiving nation is criticized.

Book publishing is yet another branch of the Western media which has come to dominate the Third World; it also, like broadcasting, reflects the drift from British to American influence. Roughly half of British annual book production is exported, nearly $\frac{1}{2}$ billion worth in 1978, most of it in educational books and material. Britain's greatest asset is her language, the use of which is growing very rapidly around the world, and her second greatest asset lies in her post-imperial connections and the fact that the educational systems of many countries are modelled on her own. However, there has been a major switch in Third World universities from the single-discipline approach of British further education to the multi-disciplinary approach of the United States. There has also been a development of indigenization of educational and especially university systems in Africa and Asia, so that the appeal of the British textbook has diminished somewhat.

It is or was the firm domestic market which enabled Britain's book exports to build up so strongly right through the century, it being particularly convenient to print at low cost extra copies of a well-established primer or text for sale overseas. The British government has long helped to subsidize textbook sales in developing countries, as a form of overseas aid, which helped a domestic industry at the same time. If American publishing or indigenous publishing were to move into large parts of the Third World book market, Britain's publishers, unlike other industries, would find it immensely hard to replace lost sales by looking to the market of the EEC, since books compete only marginally within foreign-language markets. Despite the growth in the use of English in many parts of Western Europe, it is unlikely that a market will develop there for English books which is large enough to replace that of Africa, Australia or parts of Asia, should these ever disappear. American publishers have greatly expanded in the last two decades and huge amalgamations have taken place. So we are likely to see a publishing war between the two English-speaking giants fought out in the subtly changing markets of the Third World, in which the governments of both countries may be obliged to play a part.

Since the 1940s, of course, the structure of world power has altered decisively, away from the prosperous one-third to the non-aligned, less prosperous two-thirds of the world. The voting power of the non-aligned nations was negligible at the time of the founding of the United Nations and UNESCO, but has become the decisive element in both organizations during the 1970s. UNESCO has, in fact, been the object of a kind of Third World takeover. It is from this platform that its spokesmen have launched their most powerful attacks on the spread of US and general Western cultural power.

Along with the political and economic-battles, they have attempted —perhaps paradoxically—to fight imperialism in the cultural field while demanding more of the technology through which the phenomenon of dependence has been supplied. At the heart of the argument is the implicit notion that it is possible to demand the transference of Western technology while preserving the cultural integrity of the receiving country. The early post-war ideas concerning development, enunciated by such scholars as Daniel Lerner,[16] Ithiel de Sola Pool,[17] Lucien Pye[18] and Frederick Frey[19] have been eroded; these argued that increasing urbanization would raise and was raising literacy levels, which would lead to increased use of information media which would in turn increase per capita income and an interest in democratic citizenship, thereby binding the new societies together and increasing economic prosperity. The developing countries would thus rapidly grow in the image of America and her Western

Table 2

REGIONS	DAILY PAPERS	NEWSPAPERS CIRCULATION		RADIO BROADCASTING	RECEIVERS	
	Number	Millions	Per 1,000 inhabitants	TRANSMITTERS	Millions	Per 1,000 inhabitants
WORLD[1]	7,900	408	130	25,510	218	293
Africa[2]	190	6	14	700	28	71
Asia (inc. Japan)[1,2]	2,230	90	64	2,730	108	76
Northern America	1,935	66	281	8,470	424	1,793
Latin America	1,075	23	70	4,270	78	240
Europe[3]	1,660	115	243	5,980	158	334
Oceania	120	7	305	330	6	284
USSR	690	101	396	3,030	116	455
(Arab States)	(115)	(3)	(20)	(250)	(17)	(123)
Industrialized countries	4,620	350	312	18,840	758	676
Developing countries	3,280	58	29	6,670	160	80

| REGIONS | BOOK PRODUCTION | | | | TELEVISION | | |
| | NUMBER OF TITLES | | PERCENTAGE DISTRIBUTION OF | | | RECEIVERS | |
	Thousands	Per million inhabitants	Book production	Population	TRANSMITTERS	Millions	Per 1,000 inhabitants
WORLD[1]	568	182	100	100	24,980	366	117
Africa[2]	11	27	1·9	12·8	200	2·4	6
Asia (inc. Japan)[1]	88	62	15·5	45·3	6,610	35·5	25
Northern America	92	389	16·2	7·6	4,360	131	554
Latin America	29	89	5·1	10·4	450	27	83
Europe[3]	264	558	46·1	15·1	11,250	112	237
Oceania	5	235	0·9	0·7	360	4·6	216
USSR	79	310	13·9	8·2	1,750	53	208
(Arab States)	(5)	(35)	(0·9)	(4·5)	(190)	(3·2)	(23)
Industrialized countries	388	346	68·3	35·8	23,840	327	292
Developing countries	180	90	31·7	64·2	1,140	38	19

Source: UNESCO Statistical Yearbook 1976, pp. 802, 921, 993, 1020.
Notes: (¹) Exclud. China, Dem. Peop. Rep. of Korea, Viet-Nam (²) Exclud. Arab States (³) Exclud. USSR.

democratic partners. But in practice what has happened is that Western economic models have been introduced, tying the receiving society ever closer (but in a condition of dependence) to Western companies; then came the introduction of a technology of a kind which has rendered the society helplessly expectant of Western cultural content, which has in turn 'softened up' the local élites for the further spread of Western economic patterns. The technology has been offered in a cool value-free mood, but it is quickly enveloped in ideological and political clothing of a kind rejected by many within the receiving societies.[20] That really has been the frustration behind the Third World move into UNESCO as a platform for their new cause—an insistence on cultural reciprocity with the West (and to some extent with the Soviet Union) before the transfer of further technology. But the demand raises its own contradictions which will no doubt become more and more apparent during the 1980s. The seizure of the cultural platform by the culturally dependent nations can only be one stage in an attempt to roll back the political power of the United States.

There is, therefore, a danger that a kind of cultural world war could break out with a wave of ethnic protectionism. A great deal of pure self-destructive chauvinism and autocracy could follow in the wake of campaigns for the preservation of 'national cultures', if these are defined too narrowly. Some Third World governments may be tempted towards a closing of cultural frontiers or a period of religious reaction, of the kind practised in the Ayatollah Khomeini's Iran. As Dr Pasquali, the Deputy Director General of UNESCO (a Venezualen), puts it:

> A national culture is not the touristic total of stones, heroes, folklore and fashions which characterize, roughly speaking, the national stereotype, but the synthesis of a spiritual legacy of a national community. As a common and global patrimony, it includes all the concrete and abstract values which define and characterize it.[21]

The concept of modern nationalism is deliberately anti-chauvinist. It is a movement which allows those who have been politically underprivileged to reach the self-consciousness necessary for them to act as full partners in a world society. But when it becomes an end in itself it imperils the freedom of those whom it seeks to enfranchize.

The argument about ethnic culture has a further paradox built into it, one that is inextricably involved in the general debate about mass culture in the West. Mass culture products constitute the non-élite culture of the developed countries; they are the fodder of radio, television, pulp fiction, cinema, gramophone. In the developing world it tends to be the urbanized élite which is the recipient of the exported material made originally for the Western 'mass'. In the Third World it is the 'mass', so-called, which remains tied to the ethnic culture and which is therefore comparatively immune from Western information dependence, while at the same time it is held up as the most extreme victim of Western economic expansion. That is a wide generalization and many of the more rapidly developing societies (such as Brazil) have created their own mixed genres for the popular media, partly borrowed from, say, Western soap opera, but partly based on their own traditional methods of telling stories. Japanese television has also created its own special 'eastern-westerns'. None the less, the discussion is apt to become tied in with two contradictory cultural snobbisms: the élite of East and West patronizing their respective 'masses' for opposite reasons.

One celebrated study of the importation of television into the countries of the Third World, by Elihu Katz and George Wedell,[22] has demonstrated very eloquently the importance of developing countries evolving their own models for media rather than attempting to impose those of the West. They studied the establishment of television in the 1950s and, particularly in the developing countries, discovered a vast array of exaggerated hopes, self-defeating political goals, competition between departments of government and general unpreparedness. Country after country has abandoned the structures which were set up after independence to house the media of radio and television. In Nigeria, for example,[23] the federal government was aware that it needed a national public television system to help overcome the differences of ethnic groupings, religions, language groups in a country 70–80 per cent illiterate. But it failed to plan for the diversity of local interests. The regional governments then proceeded to set up their own commercial regional stations, whose senior staff were appointed by the governor-general of Nigeria in council, but the regional economies were not ready and the stations all collapsed, their shares being handed over to the direct ownership of the regional governments. In many countries, early broadcasting systems have slipped willy-nilly into the hands of ruling groups, sometimes military groups.

By providing the software for television stations in the Third

World, the Western exporters are doing more than divert the local newly upsprung bourgeoisie; they may also be providing key assistance in the maintenance of various ruling cliques, for whom the control of broadcasting is felt to be a crucial political weapon. In Western democracies, government-controlled media are thought to be (and usually are) rejected by audiences as boring and untrustworthy, especially when a rival channel exists in the private sector. In the Third World, government-controlled media often succeed in performing an important political task, maintaining local social inequalities while boosting the credibility of unrepresentative governments.

It is possible to build up a hostile case against media exports to Third World countries on a wide range of grounds—political, financial, cultural. The universal and international trend at the present time towards the traditional, the local, the ethnic, and against gigantism of all kinds, has inevitably helped to feed the argument against unhindered media imperialism. None the less, as has been seen, a ponderous dilemma hangs over the argument at its very centre, since the case must depend upon our idea of the nature of 'development'. We do not really know whether the destruction or relegation of traditional cultures is a necessary prerequisite to the raising of living standards. We do not really understand the connection between democracy and tradition. We do not even know whether the casual application of such abstractions to the thousands of ethnic groups which make up the Third World is just another of those crude Western-imposed labels. Perhaps each one really is different. Perhaps some can easily survive the importation of a foreign culture wholesale while others cannot. Nor is there any certainty that local leaderships at any given moment are in a position to make the best practical judgement of the issue. The concept of development is as susceptible to prevailing intellectual trends as any other branch of political discussion.

Inevitably, the pursuit of economic development entails the sacrifice of some part of every traditional culture. The problem of the 1980s will be to find some way to guarantee the achievement of economic development while minimizing the disruption of cultures. In the 1960s and 1970s the cause of development proved a failure while the process of cultural dependence intensified, the receiving nations thus losing out in both fields. What this depressing experience appears to have taught the leaders of the Third World is that independence, political, economic and cultural, is the crucial prerequisite for all forms of satisfactory growth and change. Without independence in information and culture the gains of political and economic independence are rapidly eroded. But as the new technologies of communication inevitably spread deeper and deeper into the new societies it becomes ever harder to maintain local cultural autonomy. The paradoxes of dependence multiply and a political backlash results, of the kind which we are witnessing today in the international debate over the flow of news.

In starting up this North–South quarrel over the issue of information, Third World governments have been reaching out for some tangible manifestation of a felt cultural inequity. The international agencies involved in the collection and distribution of news are within easy reach of the hand of government, and so it is they who are now taking the brunt of the attack. Perhaps these governments feel they can thus acquire a firmer purchase over an otherwise intangible form of injustice.

3. News Imperialism?

The newspapers of a country are as important as symbols of its identity as its flag or currency or national anthem or the face of its head of state. *Pravda*, *Le Monde*, *The Times*, the *New York Times* and all the other papers in less common alphabets and character symbols which are seen in news-stands in major tourist centres are a kind of typographic United Nations in themselves.

On a day when important international news has broken there is an uncanny unanimity in their headlined stories, but because of their great diversity, there is a very broad spread of topics among their major stories on a normal day. Strictly speaking, the newspaper falls into a number of quite distinct international species: South American and Scandinavian newspapers reveal to this day the way in which they have developed from nineteenth-century opinion papers, often belonging directly to political parties; American newspapers clearly concentrate on local news, each of them belonging to a specific city, none of them daring to offer its readers a greater variety of national or international news than its editor fears his readers are willing to bear; British newspapers, in their efforts to maintain national audiences, are as much in the entertainment business as in inform- ation—they also still reveal the imperial past of Britain in their preoccupations with African, Indian (and also American) news; German and Austrian newspapers are clearly more concerned with the political affairs of the European continent than those of the more geographically peripheral nations. The newspaper can be the most ethnocentric of media, the one communication system which is least susceptible to the processes of 'media imperialism', keeping close to its audience which has to make the daily decision to purchase, close also to its government whose affairs it is supposed to monitor. Local transportation problems are perhaps the managers' greatest regular headache, together with the local economic circumstances which generate the advertising on which the finance of the press depends. None the less, a great controversy has broken out in recent years over the alleged dominance of newspaper content by a tiny group of international news agencies who control the market for world news.

There is a simple economic reason why so few newspapers manage to provide their international news for themselves. It costs anything up to $150,000 a year to maintain a correspondent in a foreign capital; as well as his or her salary and expenses there is the huge bill for telephone and telegraphic costs. Even in the prosperous Western world, only a handful of newspapers keep a full team of correspondents, and many of those, such as the *New York Times*, the *Washington Post*, the *Observer* and Times Newspapers eke out the costs by selling their news to other non-competing newspapers. For the newspapers of developing societies, overseas bureaux are impossible luxuries. Even where they manage to keep the odd stringer at work in London or New York, they find the telecommunications costs a crippling burden. Most international news reaches the vast majority of newspapers through a group of four large Western agencies: Reuters, Agence France-Presse, Associated Press and United Press International. Despite this concentration of the business, not one of them makes any profit to speak of from the activity of collecting and selling this information. Reuters makes its profits from services of commercial information and from its operations within North America, maintaining its ancient international news-gathering operation on the back of its other departments. The AP is cooperatively owned by its member-newspapers and merely tries to break even—although it makes a little extra cash from selling its news to radio stations. AFP is virtually subsidized by the French government, through a complex system by which the government pays the (obligatory) subscriptions to AFP of various public bodies, such as embassies, town halls, prefectures. UPI is the only out-and-out capitalistic enterprise among the world agencies, but its profits from its foreign news operations are insignificant, its revenues coming in practice from various subsidiary activities and spin-offs. It is odd, therefore, that such a torrent of opposition is being voiced against a group of organizations who appear to be performing this service as an act of public charity.

The hostility towards the world agencies stems from the feeling—or at least from the accusation—that the world agencies are principally responsible for the relationships of dependence which were discussed in the previous chapter. As the statement of the New Delhi meeting of non-aligned nations of 1976 put it:

This situation perpetuates the colonial era of dependence and domination. It confines judgements and decisions on what should be known and how it should be made known, into the hands of the few. In a situation where the means of information are domi-

nated and monopolized by a few, freedom of these few to propa-
gate information in the manner of their choosing is the virtual
denial to the rest of the right to inform and be informed objectively
and accurately.[1]

The case is further sharpened by the argument that there is a special
Western concept of news which tends to oblige Western journalists
to seek the aberrational rather than the normal as the main criterion
for selection; Western news agencies are, therefore, on the lookout
for information concerning violence, war, crime, corruption, disaster,
famine, fire, flood. The resulting flow of information therefore
systematically distorts international knowledge of the cultural,
political and economic progress of the Third World and emphasizes
its negative aspects. The vexation is further exacerbated by the fact
that the Third World, like the rest, is obliged to receive its news (i.e.,
news about itself) only after it passes through the distorting mechanism of the four Western news agencies. There are, of course, major
news agencies in the socialist world, such as Tass and Novosti, Hsin
Hua and Ceteka, but these have adopted a different ideology of news
to correspond with their different political ideology and, in any case,
are not in practice major sources of daily information about economic
and political developments in the major industrialized societies.
(Tass supplies a great deal of information gratis about the socialist
world as a whole.) The case against the Western agencies cannot be
dismissed and is certainly of considerable importance as a phenomenon in itself. The roots of the inequalities in the flow of news lie
very deep in the past and in the historical processes which have been
discussed earlier.

Let us take, for example, the newspapers of South America, which
from 1870 until 1920 were completely dependent upon Havas, a
French news agency now defunct, for the whole of their flow of news
from the outside world. Havas had done a deal with Reuters of
Britain and Wolff of Germany—the only other world agencies of any
importance in the latter half of the last century—by which the world
was carved up between the three of them. In 1920, the United Press
Association (which, after a merger with another agency, only became
United Press International or UPI in 1937) broke through the Havas
monopoly in South America and started to provide news about the
US direct to *La Prensa* of Buenos Aires, and soon to other Latin
American papers. Gradually, United Press and its competitor the
AP (which is an agency owned by the principal clients among

American metropolitan dailies) took over the South American news market, though to this day there remains a powerful French linkage and also an important British link through Reuters. But newspapers throughout Latin America are deeply impregnated with an American attitude to news, very different though this is from that tradition of the Latin American press which stems from the ideological debates of nineteenth-century nationalism. Fifty per cent of world news published in the papers of South America comes from the two US agencies and a further 10 per cent emanates from Reuters and the modern successor of Havas, the Agence France-Presse. The total amount of news taken by the principal papers of this continent from news agencies owned by countries which are members of the Third World amounts only to a few percentage points.

There are, of course, many national news agencies in South America but they have never been able to muster the resources to commence a continental, still less an international, service of their own. LATIN has recently come into existence and operates in a number of South American countries, but it has been created by Reuters and obtains its material through Reuters. No daily paper in certain Latin American countries maintains a single overseas correspondent even in the neighbouring capital city. So deeply has the US news culture established itself in the continent that there seems no point in creating a major new agency to feed the continent's press: it would only duplicate the services already provided from the north, since North and South American papers have come to share the same news values, or so say many of the journalists who work in the principal dailies of the region.

A Mexican researcher has done an interesting analysis of the coverage of the granting of independence to Surinam.[2] Not one paper in the same continent of the world sent a correspondent to cover the event. Surinam, although a neighbour, was not thought to be an 'important' news source, even at so dramatic a point in its history. The press of Latin America operates in a 'receive-only' mode towards the world's news and it accepts the world-view of its principal supplier. Or so it appears. A country which seems peripheral or irrelevant to American journalists will be treated in the same way by the journalists of the whole of South America, even if that country happens to be one of themselves. On 26 November 1975, not one Latin American paper even carried Surinam's independence story on its front page, although the world-famous Brazilian daily *O Estado* provided three columns of agency copy on an inside page—a good New York murder would fare better. What was perhaps more revealing and more worrying was that the material which was published on this event reflected the view of American journalists (who originated the material) that Surinam was incapable of governing herself and had racial conflicts looming up.

Third World papers pay as much attention to the private lives of American celebrities, to the dangers of another San Francisco earthquake, to the problems of drug-taking among American students, to the health of the American president, as they do to the comparable personalities and issues of their own societies. The news sent out from Latin America, Africa and Asia to the international agencies is sent by local agency offices and representatives who are often natives of the countries concerned. Yet the local journalist will send the New York office the material which he knows it wants; this is then retransmitted with the agencies' bulletins to the newspapers of the same region according to the presumed news priorities of those papers. There is, in other words, a vicious circle, whereby news values are developed by the news agencies, then revalidated by reference to the buying public (which seems quite content with not being fed with worrying news about its own sector of the globe—the normal reports of catastrophe and instability in the Third World being confined to other countries) then fed back into the receiving paper as the perceived 'demand' of the reading public concerned. What the agency in effect generates is a dependence upon what it offers, which it satisfies by means of local journalists 'trained' to fit the mould. Agency head offices, local reporters, local editors and reading public are caught within a closed circle of practices and assumptions about the nature of news.

In very recent years an attempt has been made to inject fresh sources of material into South American papers and, on the part of the papers themselves, to treat agency material with more circumspection. But for the closed circle of news values to be truly opened up will take a major effort, for it is ultimately the perceived taste of the reading public which has to be changed; newspapers will not in any continent go far beyond their readers' believed needs. Readers and editors have to see for themselves that the old news values cannot achieve the kinds of insight into a society which that society itself requires. Conferring newsworthiness upon the traditionally unnewsworthy entails, among other things, shaking the faith of professionals in the relevance and reliability of their own professional training.

The five agencies which supply international news in bulk—AP, UPI, Reuters, AFP plus the Soviet Union's Tass—have all emerged from the imperial and post-imperial competition of the last century, by which great powers tried to spread their news networks throughout the areas of their economic and political suzerainty. Between them these agencies today have nearly 50,000 clients spread around the globe (although by no means evenly spread). Their information, which was once supplied by morse or crackling telephone wires, today pours through microwave and satellite links, passing through high-speed wires at the rate of 1,200 or more words per minute. All of the agencies use modern video-terminals and computer storage of their material. The four Western agencies send out, between them, 34 million words per day and claim to provide nine-tenths of the entire foreign news output of the free world's newspapers, radio and television stations. The AP alone claims to reach one-third of the world every day.

Although many of the other 120 agencies operating in the world are very large in themselves, they are very far from being able to rival the five giants. It is these five organizations which lie at the heart of the contemporary international wrangle over 'news flow' and whether it is or should be 'free' and whether it ought, in certain senses, to be 'balanced'. Their network of correspondents is by no means geographically balanced in terms of locations of work. Taking the world agencies together (i.e., including Tass), 34 per cent of their correspondents are kept in the United States alone, 28 per cent in Europe (east and west), 17 per cent in Asia and Australia, 11 per cent in Latin America, 6 per cent in the Middle East and 4 per cent in Africa. Of course, one may argue that these statistics reflect the location of the news. And the agencies could certainly argue that, whatever the imbalances in the location of their correspondents, their Third World offices are still run at a loss and that they are in effect subsidizing their Third World news-gathering operations: AP for example, collects only 1 per cent of its revenue from the Third World as a whole, yet spends 5 per cent or more of its revenue on collecting news from the Third World.

It is impossible, when looking at the evolution of these organizations, to fail to perceive in them the shadow of the structure of the capitalist system itself. For capitalism was an information system, as well as a financial and productive system; its development necessitated bringing one unexploited part of the world after another into a single market in which social classes, companies, transportation methods and stock markets became inextricably combined into a single, complicated and variegated, ever-growing and interdependent system. At the heart of it there had to be information, for the central concept of capitalism is the market and, in a global system, physical markets have to be replaced by notional markets or vicarious markets in which prices and values are assessed through the distribution of regular reliable information. The communications network which grew up in the nineteenth century was one outcome of the imperial system, by which competing capitalist powers fought for more of the world in which to operate a privileged trading system; at the same time, the information network was a fundamental support for the development of international capitalism itself—it was, that is, both the cause and the result of capitalism.

It was no accident, then, that the same nations which controlled physical transportation around the globe and which thereby maintained contact with their centres of trade and their colonies, also constructed the first news networks to sell information to the world's newspapers. The traders and overseas administrators, like the explorers before them, were in themselves the basic sources of knowledge of the world and it was their view which was implicit in imperial society's creation of the political realities of the globe. Europe was the centre of the universe and the rest of the world had been progressively 'discovered'. In its service, whole peoples could be shifted from one continent to another to provide cheap labour where it was unavailable naturally. Europe was gripped by an extraordinary ethnocentric arrogance which overlay its collective mind so completely that it has not even yet worn away, despite the tremendous political shocks of the twentieth century. All that Europe knew about Africa, for example, was and is still culled from its own economically interested encounters with it. Thus whole civilizations have existed in that continent which have hardly entered the school textbooks; but those ports and deserts and jungles which have been the scene of historical events affecting Europe in some way have entered the European imagination as if they were the stuff of salient *African* history.

The systems of transportation and information were essential elements in the process of defining the relationships between the two parties, colonizer and colonized, within the imperial system. Shipping services and trains brought the two groups into contact; they did not bring the colonized group back to Europe, except in very special conditions (and at a much later date). Colonization was not perceived to be a form of 'immigration', but a natural historical act. A generation of explorer-adventurer-reporters grew up, 'gentlemen followers' of colonial wars, half-spies for London and Paris, half-entertainers for the new reading public whose imagination was fired by accounts of their exploits. At the same time, a flow of accurate statistical information was needed to enable the processes of investment to take place. The passage of information depended upon the good and efficient maintenance of the lines of physical transport, which were organized to facilitate carriage of goods, people and information back to European (and, later, American) cities rather than to develop the colonial societies' trading among themselves. Submarine cables naturally followed shipping routes, roads connected to the ports, telegraph lines developed alongside the railway tracks. Britain's own imperial links were so stretched in the mid-nineteenth century that the government in London seized upon every possible device to facilitate trade and communication. Even before 1860, when the telegraph was still a relatively new invention, attempts were made to link Britain with the East Indies by cable; in the event India was reached by 1864. A combination of private capital and official encouragement eventually brought about the interconnection of the Empire, the All-Red Route which was not really complete until the eve of the Great War, by which time wireless telegraph was ready to perform a parallel task.

In the meantime, the European news agencies built up their news routes and branch offices throughout that part of the colonial world which was being 'opened up'. The invention of the news agency was the most important single development in the newspaper industry of the early nineteenth century, apart perhaps from the rotary press. It altered the whole scope of news dissemination, although for some decades after its inception (in the 1830s) there were newspapers, such as *The Times* of London, that preferred to continue to collect the whole of their own intelligence by means of directly employed agents. However, in 1835 Charles Havas, a French entrepreneur, acquired the Correspondence Garnier, a news bureau dealing mainly in the translation of foreign papers, and began to transform it into a new kind of information business. The news sources continued to be the published newspapers of the rest of Europe in addition to the special newsletters disseminated by bureaux operating at the major business centres of the continent. The initiation of the telegraph in the next decade made it possible for clients outside France to receive Havas's information services and two of his employees, Paul Julius Reuter and

Bernhard Wolff, proceeded to found parallel services in England and Germany (though Reuter at first tried to squeeze into the French market before settling in London). It was clear almost from the start that the news agency business was basically a national monopoly affair, there being great difficulty for any second company to establish itself within a single national market.

So rapidly was the demand for commercial information increasing —on businesses, stocks, currencies, commodities, harvests, extractive products—in the middle of the nineteenth century, that the news business never faltered. Each political shift, every insurrection and revolution, occasioned a flurry in the money markets and the swift communication of fresh events was a most valuable service. At first the skill lay in the construction of private networks of physical links: Reuter used pigeons and horses to join the ends of the various cable systems and he and Wolff set up their contacts around central Europe to provide the quickest possible flow of intelligence. At the time of the 1851 Exhibition a cable was laid between London and the continent and Reuter saw his chance to spread his network of contacts and sell their information onwards from the biggest business centre in the world.

Reuter and his rivals were intent upon expanding their information businesses, as fast as the development of cable or other methods of transport made it possible to expedite the intelligence culled from the different business centres. Reuter established a hegemony in the Low Countries and then moved eastwards to Vienna, Athens and the Black Sea. The private telegraph companies had in the meantime built their services out to India but decided to collect news for themselves in that market and retail it to Europe (something they were eventually forbidden to do at home or abroad). Reuter provided so admirable a service in London that the British government agreed to allow him to use its own telegrams from India as a source of news, thereby enabling him to break the exclusivity of the telegraph companies. Reuter's service thus acquired an aura of semi-officialdom.[3]

The Times, however, had created a separate network of intelligence in Europe, which it refused to dismantle. To them it was inconceivable to print reports from anyone other than their own staff. Reuter, unable, therefore, to sell his service in what was, until well into the 1860s, by far the largest single news supplier in London, concentrated on building a clientele among the provincial papers and smaller London dailies. New papers sprang up in immense numbers in the last quarter of the century outside London and Reuter's service could supply them with most of the foreign news they needed at some-times little more than a pound a week.

Reuter thus very quickly found himself supplying two very distinct markets: on the one hand the trading community requiring instant, exact and copious commercial and political information, on the other a large number of smaller newspapers whose readers wanted romantic headlines, big stories and not too much substance. For the latter, war coverage was the most treasured commodity. Editors had been featuring battle news since the French Revolution and even earlier, but the telegraph helped to bring into existence a specialized sub-division of reporters dealing in war information. William Howard Russell had made his name in the Crimean War and Forbes Robert-son laid out the journalistic principles of war reporting in the 1870s. The war reporter exercised an important political role (as well as something of a military one) because of his ability to reach the emotions of tens of thousands of readers and provide them with the imagery of the Empire—since the majority of available wars were linked with its development. Reuter continued to expand and even before the Franco-Prussian War he had succeeded in laying a cable around the north of Germany and linking it to the telegraph which ran down through Russia via the Persian Gulf to India. The whole of the Middle East lay open to him and he could already see onwards to Australia via the Far East. The public acclaim which accrued from the reporting of spectacular events energized the government to help smooth the diplomatic paths towards the goal of worldwide cover-age.

The rivalry of the major powers of Europe, however, tended to hinder the free expansion of their respective national news agencies, all three of which enjoyed political patronage, although Havas and Wolff were more closely linked in their activities to the policies of their respective governments. The three agencies were destined to co-operate or fight. At first they co-operated and in 1856 agreed to exchange stock market prices in their respective capital city bourses and later this was extended to political news. Reuter's movements on the continent, however, alarmed Wolff, who obtained bank finance after the personal intervention of the Prussian monarch and set up a rival commercial service, although Reuter continued to look for clients under the nose of the new Wolff agency. The three agencies saw that only a new agreement would save them from damaging mutual poaching and the only form of agreement possible was to ascribe to each a parish which corresponded with the existing

sphere of economic influence of their respective protective governments. Reuter 'obtained' at the resulting agreement of 1869 (the
Agency Alliance Treaty) the whole of Britain's empire and the entire
Far East; Havas 'received' Italy, Spain, the French and Portuguese
empires; Wolff was furnished with the less lucrative areas of Austria
and her peripheral territories, plus Scandinavia and Russia. Reuter
and Havas agreed to move into South America jointly and share the
proceeds, although eventually Havas acquired the whole of this
continent.[4]

The effect of this procedure on the new news-dependent countries
is of some interest. One may cite the case of Scandinavia. In 1866,
Eric Nikolai Ritzau, originally a German, set up a telegram agency
in Denmark, following the model of Havas, Reuter and Wolff. A
telegraph line had been open to Copenhagen already for a dozen
years, and four Danish newspapers had a joint reporting office in
Hamburg to feed the information. Ritzau set up his own office in
Hamburg and tried to obtain a direct news source in London with
the help of Reuter, who refused to co-operate. Eventually, Ritzau
built a link with Wolff and obtained his foreign news by that means.
Meanwhile, Wolff and Ritzau jointly set up an agency in Sweden,
Svenska Telegrambyran, and at the same time a Norwegian office,
the Norsk Telegrambyra, was inaugurated, which obtained its intelligence from Copenhagen and Stockholm.

In 1889, all three Scandinavian agencies agreed to exchange
domestic information gratis, in a miniature version of the great concordat concluded by the three European majors. They thus all
became clients of Wolff. Because of the 1869 agreement and his own
involvement with them, the three agencies had to rely on Wolff for
all their foreign news, as well as becoming mutually dependent,
without at first having wished to be exclusively tied to one source.
All foreign news coming into Scandinavia was thus Germanized.
Indeed, the semi-official cartel system which functioned until 1914
was one of the great influences on the development of public opinion
in countries which became involved in the First World War. Finland,
unlike her neighbours, was a client state of Russia and was permitted
to receive foreign news only through St Petersburg. The Finnish
Agency established in 1919 was permitted to have links with both
Wolff and Reuters as well as with all of the Scandinavian agencies.[5]

The great agencies were able to play crucial roles in the international micro-systems of advancing capitalism. Reuter built his
eastern empire, for example, originally on the cotton trade. He

supplied British merchants right through the East with data on harvests and production of cotton in India. His political information on China and the rest of the region was added to his specialist information on cotton and then he was able to construct within India a local sub-continental network which both collected information for his other clients and laid the foundations of an Indian press industry. In the case of Persia, Reuter even contracted to build not only the national telegraph system itself, but also a railway from the Caspian to the Persian Gulf plus branch lines. Around this enterprise he planned to develop a large series of transport-dependent industries: timber, minerals, agriculture. The Shah even gave him permission to operate the state customs system for twenty years. The British government disliked the plan, however, fearing the value of the railway to the increasingly powerful Russian state which was expanding southwards, and instructed the parties concerned to abandon it.

The agencies have a long history of sensational reporting of the Third World. *The Times* engaged the services of the Dalziel Agency, long ago defunct, to supply it with this newly needed commodity. From the 1890s it seemed that the more distant parts of the globe were permanently subject to violence and drama; the East was constantly ablaze with revolt and carnage, Central America was wracked with picturesque revolution while Africa was the province of romantic jungle explorers. Reuters started their Special Service to rival that of Dalziel, which was to deal with 'sudden and unforeseen occurrences', such as wrecks and disasters, crimes and assassinations. Reuters realized that a new market had opened up which a news agency was required to fill and which would be neglected only at its peril. The popular press consumed vast quantities of material and was beginning to expand at a tremendous rate. The mass audience was coming to birth and its appetite would be all but insatiable; its taste had to be identified, trained to the available supply and satisfied. Reuters' control of the central networks of news meant that it had to play a crucial role in this entirely new form of business. As the press was established in the settler countries of Australia, India and South Africa, Reuters was to play an important role in the exportation of British indigenous popular taste to the communities of British people in other continents.

Reuters succeeded in supplying these communities even where, as in South Africa, European settlers were divided politically among themselves. Its detachment thus became an increasingly important attribute of the service. In the case of South Africa, Reuters remained the national news agency until the outbreak of the Second World War and is of course still today the principal supplier of its foreign news. (In the past it was responsible for the entire communications network of that country.) Reuters' pre-eminence among the agencies depended upon its relative independence from the government, so long as this remained possible, and its ability to command credibility among the many groups and interests which made up the Empire.

Wolff's position in Germany and Havas's in France were rather different and increasingly reflective of their geo-political positions. In the years leading up to the Great War they became ever more dependent upon their respective governments, although continuing their role in the three-agency cartel. It was with the outbreak of war and the sequestration of its foreign holdings that Reuters also found itself needing assistance from the British government. The agency divided its services into two sections, one supplying news to neutral countries, the other serving the domestic network of clients. Reuters' famed detachment disappeared when its managing director was appointed director of propaganda during the war—to run concurrently with his task at Reuters—leading observers to the conclusion that the agency, like its counterparts in Europe, had merely become a tool of government. Reuters' messages clearly contained material which emanated from the pen of the War Cabinet, in addition to its normal material.

Yet despite the general crippling of agency credibility during the war, the market for news increased very considerably. The newspaper world in general benefited from the surge of popular interest in international events while newspapers in the post-war period increased their coverage of commercial news, which Reuters was well equipped to supply. Though it suffered a severe blow to its pride and credibility as a result of criticism of its conduct during the war, it was able to identify new markets for its material in the 1920s and reestablish its independence of the government in London.

The great change which the war brought to the world of news agencies was the introduction of the two American agencies to the international communications scene. These two agencies had had very different origins, Associated Press having been established as a non-profit co-operative among a group of six New York newspapers as far back as 1848, while the United Press Association had been founded in 1907 as a privately owned enterprise (by E. W. Scripps and passed on to his dynasty) in order to break the monopoly of the

AP. AP's policy, until it was declared unconstitutional in 1943, was to admit new members only with the agreement of existing members, which in practice meant that only one publishing house per city or per market was eligible. Scripps deliberately broke through this barrier and established his own news organization which would sell to any newspaper at all. From 1893 onwards AP had been a member, in its own right, of the European cartel, whereby Reuters gave up its right to distribute news within the United States and its overseas possessions to AP while the latter supplied the European agencies with news from America. Scripps's agency started to set up its own offices in South America and elsewhere and used the international communications network (owned by the British company Exchange Telegraph) to sell news to Japanese and to South American newspapers.[6]

In the aftermath of the war the whole distribution of world power was seen to be transformed. The two American agencies were determined to break out of the web of isolationism. AP had discovered the agreement of 1893 to be a positive liability when all three European agencies were known to have acted as direct tools of government. It had used their obvious bias to develop contacts in neutral countries during the First World War. AP's restlessness was clear to Reuters, which tried at first to switch loyalties to the rival UPA, but Scripps was determined to continue building his new agency into a world power in its own right and would not agree to confine his news-collecting activities to the American domestic scene. During much of the war, South America had been under an effective news blockade and its links with Havas had been tenuous. AP and UPA had both built their links to the major Latin American newspapers and continued to strengthen these ties in the 1920s, despite their formal adherence to the rules of the cartel.[6]

The two American agencies found room for expansion in the Far East as well, as American economic interests were developed in that region; Reuters needed the East as an area of expansion to replace its European markets lost during the war and within the borders of the British Empire its position was secure. Japan, however, was a different matter; Reuters had enjoyed a news monopoly (inwards and outwards) in the Japanese Empire since 1870, but in 1926 it was forced officially to concede AP the right to have direct dealings with the national Japanese agency (Kokusai), which had been an exclusive partner of Reuters. UPA, however, was free to compete in Japan, since it was not subject to any limiting agreements, and AP, fearing the results of competition conducted unevenly between itself and its rival in the American news market, sought to gain further concessions from Reuters. In the early 1930s, AP started to make direct news arrangements with the Japanese agency and Reuters responded by renouncing the agreement between the three European agencies and AP. From 1934 onwards, AP and its rivals had a free hand both to collect and distribute news anywhere in the world. The sharing of spheres of influence between the agencies was at an end and an era of open competition began. The inherited zones of influence, nevertheless remained, and each agency sought to maximize the advantages of the markets with which history had endowed it. Although Havas disappeared as a news agency as a result of the Second World War (it had collaborated with the Vichy regime) and was replaced by a new agency, the Agence France-Presse, the new AFP absorbed the traditions and assets of its predecessor (the AFP was a merger of two free French agencies which had been formed by staff who had left Havas after its collaboration). Wolff had finally disappeared into the maw of the Nazi regime and with the division of Germany at the end of the war there was no chance of a German news agency—East or West—reconstructing the influence of Wolff. Its Russian sphere had of course disappeared and a new Soviet agency, Tass, grew up in the 1950s and 1960s as a major world institution. The agency of the German Federal Republic, the Deutsche Presse Agentur (DPA), has built a massive presence for itself throughout all of Europe, as well as Africa and other continents, but its activities still fall a long way short of world agency status.[7]

The evolution of Tass is a subject of some historical interest. Russia had been assigned to Wolff under the Agency Alliance Treaty, a fact which mirrored the political relations between these two countries (later expressed in the secret Russo-German defence treaty of 1887). Russia's later decision to align with France did not upset the news relationship between Germany and Russia, even when France signed a secret defence treaty with the Tsar in 1890 and started to subsidize his regime. France was simply sticking to the terms of the concordat and indeed continued to support the link between Wolff and the Russian Telegraph Agency, which was founded in 1894. Russian bankers and officials, however, were less than happy with the arrangement and suspected Wolff of deliberately withholding important financial information because of the growing tension. In the years leading up to the First World War the Tsarist regime created a new agency, the St Petersburg Telegraph Agency, provided it with funds and placed it under direct governmental tutelage, and it was this organization which the Bolsheviks took over in 1917, placing it alongside the Press Bureau of the All-Russian Central Executive of Workers', Peasants' and Soldiers' Deputies. In the first year of the revolution there was considerable conflict between the two bodies and soon they merged into ROSTA (Russian Tele-graph Agency), with two departments, one for news and the other for propaganda. ROSTA made agreements with UPA but broke away again after a time when disagreements broke out between Reuters and UPA, since ROSTA wished to have friendly relations with Great Britain. When the Soviet Union was declared in 1925, the new agency Tass emerged from ROSTA and this body, in the 1930s, renounced the cartel and made agreements with both American agencies. Lenin and all the early Bolsheviks wrote for ROSTA, whose purpose was avowedly to agitate as well as inform.

Tass set out originally to become a world agency in the inter-war years. Its correspondents began to settle in the major news centres of the world and when the war came a large group of war correspondents were sent into the field, when the agency also re-verted to its 'agit-prop' role. Its attitude to news is clearly quite different, and has always been, from that of the other major agencies. It exists to serve the interests of the Soviet state and was tutored from its earliest days in the Leninist art of polemic, the art of struggle. Unlike the other agencies, it proclaims that it exists to form public opinion, to orientate the people 'correctly' and to do so with infor-mation which is topical and truthful, but 'socially meaningful' at the same time. It is directly responsible to the Council of Ministers of the USSR and, in a statement to UNESCO, defined its own role over-seas as being 'to systematically explain to foreign readers the peace-loving foreign policy of the CPSU and the Soviet government . . . disseminate information about the achievements of real socialism in economy, science and culture, publicize the Soviet way of life, expose the concoctions and slander of the bourgeois ideology . . .'

Today, Tass's general director is appointed by the Praesidium of the Central Committee and all its international contracts and agree-ments have to pass through the Ministry of Foreign Affairs. Tass operates on the basis of subscription fees from 3,000 Soviet news-papers plus thousands of non-media clients. Its services reach foreign media free of charge, which causes many Third World papers to take advantage of them. Tass reached the height of its influence in the aftermath of the Second World War as it took over the agencies of the defunct Deutsches Nachrichtenbureau of the Hitler regime in Eastern Europe. Until the Iron Curtain descended in the 1950s, Tass had to compete in Eastern Europe with the Western agencies, but as the communist regimes established themselves Tass became a major force in Eastern Europe. Meanwhile, the agencies which had flourished under the Austro-Hungarian Empire gave way to the new national agencies of the Eastern European satellite countries; Tass had acted as a major source of information to the wartime resistance forces in those countries and the new national agencies began to draw more and more of their news from it rather than from AP, UPA and Reuters. In 1961, the Union of Journalists and Writers established Novosti, the Soviet Union's other agency. Its purpose is to circulate essays by public figures to subscribing periodicals, including newspapers, throughout the world.

The general spread of Tass around the world has declined in the 1960s and 1970s, especially as a result of the growing authority of the Chinese agency Hsin Hua (founded in 1929 as the Red China News Agency) in many parts of the world. It is also fair to say that Tass lost a great deal more of its authority simply as a result of its poor service and low reliability.

The four non-communist world agencies are all different from one another in significant structural ways. Reuters continues to do most of its business in the sphere of economic and financial news. It is not a national agency (that role is performed in Britain by another co-operative agency, the Press Association). It is international only. The supplying of newspapers with information represents about a quarter of its turnover, and is not even one of the company's major profit centres. The discontent surrounding Reuters in the aftermath of the First World War evaporated with the creation of a new structure of ownership of the agency. Reuters is today a trust owned not by government nor by a private company, but by all of the press of the United Kingdom, national and provincial, and by the newspaper associations of Australia, New Zealand and the Republic of Ireland. It is not run for the purposes of maximizing profits, but of serving its members.

AP is also a non-profit co-operative, but its members are all purely American newspapers and the income of the agency, 80 per cent of it at least, is drawn from American radio, television and domestic press. Its six directors are appointed at annual members' meetings. Overseas clients are non-media clients and relatively unimportant to its finances—a contrast with Reuters, which sees itself as an international organization, owning no particular loyalty to a single nation, government or medium.

UPI is a more aggressively commercial body, though it has not returned a dividend for two decades and has experienced certain financial difficulties in the 1970s owing to the immense cost of technological advance. UPI continues to be owned by the Scripps Company, which also owns the Scripps-Howard newspapers, the United Feature Syndicate, as well as various broadcasting enterprises. Since 1957, when UPI altered its name, it has contained a small interest on the part of the Hearst family, which merged its International News Service with the old UPA.

AFP was reconstructed in 1957 to present a non-governmental face to the world; its revenues are drawn entirely from its subscriptions and it therefore claims to operate independently and purely commercially—but a vast proportion of its revenues is, as has been explained, paid by the French authorities. From time to time senior civil servants are appointed to important jobs within the AFP. The other agencies do not regard it as a politically independent body, despite its claims. Its Administrative Council (which chooses the chief executive—a président directeur général) has fifteen members, representing French radio, television, newspapers, the client public services and the staff.

Although the dissimilarities of structure and purpose between these large institutions of the developed (though not just the capitalist) world are considerable, the great division in the world of agencies is between these and the 120 other national and special agencies. Today almost every developed country has an agency of its own. Ireland and Canada do not. Altogether, there are forty countries in the world with seats at the UN but no national news agency. Two dozen of these have populations above a million. There are also hundreds of specialist agencies, which deal in scientific news or special business services or bring information to tourists, economists, sports fans; some of them have been set up to carry political messages, both national and international—in Scandinavia several political parties have their own agencies sending out political speeches and statements to newspapers with the same political coloration. Of these many are co-operatives or non-profit bodies, though among the national agencies the majority are directly controlled by a minister; they do, however, maintain contracts with one or more of the five major world agencies, all of which operate in at least 100 countries on a round-the-clock basis, issuing their material in a variety of languages.

In Europe, every country, apart from seven very small ones, has an agency. All of them receive a flow of news from one or more of the international agencies, as well as with the national agencies of neighbouring countries. They nearly all have at least some correspondents stationed abroad, Germany's DPA and Italy's ANSA enjoying a complement of correspondents almost large enough to rank as transnational agencies. Within Europe, various groupings exist among the agencies which hold some political significance.

In November 1938, a meeting of agencies of neutral states took place in Oslo which discussed with alarm the way in which the agencies of states on the verge of becoming belligerents were starting to adopt very partisan positions in their coverage. These neutrals started to exchange news among themselves and eighteen months later, in 1940, another grouping was formed, the Hellcommune, between the agencies of the Nordic countries, plus Holland, Belgium and Switzerland; it was shut down soon after the German invasions but renewed its links in 1945 and admitted Austria to membership in 1956. Known as Group '39, it continues to exchange news and technical expertise but has never lived up to the hopes originally invested in it: that it would contribute to the presentation of news something that was distinctively derived from a common European cultural background. Apart from sport and photographic services, the group has not been able to contribute anything novel to the editorial work of its members, although the Nordic agencies cooperating among themselves have been able to create a sense of common Nordic culture and history in the flavouring of their news.

In the 1970s, one of the most significant developments has been the arrival of a series of co-operative enterprises stretching beyond national boundaries. In due course it may turn out that these will influence the whole culture of news more profoundly than any other single phenomenon—though they are still in their infancy. In 1964, a group of journalists who favoured political and social reform in South America (though not bound together by a single narrow political claim) came together to form the Inter Press Service. A decade later the English-speaking islands in the Caribbean, with help from the UN Development Programme and UNESCO, founded the Caribbean News Agency (CANA) in conjunction with Reuters; it has now gone independent, with seventeen member institutions. An Asian regional agency has been planned since 1977 when a Colombo meeting of Asian news agencies decided to conduct a feasibility study. Since 1975, the non-aligned nations have been working together in a pool—not a collective agency—which takes material from forty national agencies and sends it out again through thirteen of them which act as redistribution points; the initiative for this venture was taken by the Yugoslav agency Tanjug which houses the pool in Belgrade.

In Africa, agencies have developed very slowly, the obstacle mainly being the poor telecommunication links which still hamper inter-connection between different parts of the continent and the outside world. To date, twenty-five African countries have established their own agencies, although the largest African state of all, Nigeria, has none of its own. In practice, they concentrate more on conveying information to radio and television stations, rather than to news-papers, and not one of them has a correspondent anywhere outside its own borders. For outside news they rely entirely upon the big five.

The position in the Middle East, as might be expected, is rather different. The eighteen agencies of the Arab states contain no fewer than five which have some international activity. The Middle East News Agency, established in Cairo, has correspondents in eleven countries in the Arab world, as well as in major European capitals. The Tunisian agency TAP also has bureaux outside Tunisia and acts as a redistribution centre for the Non-Aligned News Pool, as well as being a link with the Inter Press Service. The Arab Revolutionary News Agency (ARNA) operates across a broader spectrum of states, with a Paris correspondent in addition to radio links with Europe, Africa and North America.

In Latin America there exist only a dozen agencies among two dozen countries. Chile and Mexico have a few overseas correspon-dents but no others do. The Spanish national agency EFE supplies a certain amount of news, in addition to the big internationals. Mexico has three privately owned companies with correspondents, or at least stringers, in a number of countries. In Buenos Aires there are the offices of two previously mentioned organizations, LATIN, founded by a group of more prestigious Latin American newspapers, but managed by Reuters, and the Inter Press Service. Although the conti-nent is inadequately supplied with local agencies it is very well supplied with newspapers; perhaps because the national develop-ment of many of the countries of the continent took place in the last century, there are many newspapers of ancient lineage, in addition to hundreds of radio and television stations.

In Asia, Singapore and Hong Kong act as major international news centres. Eight major agencies have offices in Hong Kong and four in Singapore, where there are also no fewer than sixty foreign correspondents from around the world. Despite the problems occasioned by the multitude of languages, the impossibility of teletyping in many of the local scripts, the appalling scarcity of telecommunications facilities and the tiny circulation of newspapers, Asia is well supplied with national agencies. Only two or three nations, and they the very newest and smallest, lack an agency. The great range of political formulae among Asian nations means that the agencies are very wide-ranging in character, from China's Hsin Hua to Japan's Kyodo and Iran's Pars. Hsin Hua is in the process of becoming an important international agency in its own right since it now has 200 employees in forty overseas locations and a number of important bureaux in London, Paris, Geneva, New York, etc. Japan has two competing agencies, both founded in the immediate aftermath of the Second World War: Kyodo has forty-seven offices outside the country and Jiji has thirty-one; both have contracts with the major Western agencies and Kyodo with Tass as well.

Many of the Third World national agencies of today have already acquired a history as romantic, though more tragic in many ways, than any of the major world agencies. One may cite, as a striking example, AZaP, the Agence Zaire-Presse, whose predecessor came into existence a few weeks after the Congo was declared independent in the summer of 1960. It found itself immediately in the midst of the intricate and bloody turmoil which marked the first years of the Congo (Leopoldville), as it was known until the name was changed to Zaire. Its true origins go back to 1927, when the first telegraph link was established between Lubumbashi (then called Elisabethville) and Brussels. A small Belgian agency took over the management of this enterprise from the cable company and for twenty years transmitted news to and from Belgium. It was called Prescobel and survived until Belga, the Belgian national agency, took it over after the war and started a teleprinter service of news which was of considerable importance over the next ten years when newspapers sprang up in many parts of the colony. In the late 1950s, the agency was sending out a daily teleprinted bulletin in addition to the roneoed sheets of international news which it used to mail to its client newspapers. It was still a few years before Reuters and AFP were both able to supply news to Kinshasa (then called Leopoldville) via Belga in Brussels.

The agency which was set up by decree after independence was at first called the Agence Congolaise de Presse (ACP). It attempted, with the scanty paraphernalia left to it by the departing colonial administration, to become a national information centre, collecting and disseminating news about the new nation which it represented. The country, however, was engulfed in a many-sided conflict and the agency went through five directors in its first three years and ended up in 1963 with its budget slashed, its teleprinter circuit cut off and its sixth director a functionary of the Ministry of Information. The chaos lasted for a further two years until the whole country was relaunched with a new constitution and head of state. Reuters sent technicians late in 1965 to reopen the closed circuits and a Belgian organization, Inbel, reestablished its administration. During the Mobutu period the agency has continued to function in a more stable political setting, with a subscription budget supported by government subsidy, and staff of over 300.

AZaP has bilateral agreements with many other African and Third World agencies, and is also active within the Union of African News Agencies, but its technical operation is severely hampered within Zaire because of the scarcity of telephone lines between the capital and outlying cities. Much of its internal operation, therefore, has to be carried out in morse code and is dependent on the goodwill of the local operators. Reports frequently have to be carried by private travellers. Within the capital, two-way contact with the main news centres (airport, office of the president, etc.) is conducted by means of walkie-talkie sets to the central newsroom, although there are, of course, also telephones. It has a number of radio transmitters in the regions, which it lacks the maintenance staff to keep up to full standard. It also lacks sufficient trained reporters for the tasks it has set itself; at present it has one correspondent in Angola and no others in Africa at all, although it has representatives in Paris, Brussels and Peking. In its report to the MacBride Commission, AZaP complained that its correspondents were discriminated against in relation to those of larger agencies when they attempted to interview politicians or otherwise carry out their mission in many European capitals; it also complained that 'unchecked' news about Zaire was regularly published abroad, detrimental to the interests of the country.

The conditions which agencies like AZaP have had to endure during the first decades of a nation's existence mean that it has inevitably been deprived of automatic credibility in the developed world. Despite the help and training offered by the well-established agencies to the new African ones, the sheer political maze in which they have to live means that the stern ideals of such as Paul Julius

Reuter are difficult to pursue. Such agencies, when confronting their problems, perhaps feel they are being first robbed and then preached at, rather than assisted. To establish a tradition of fair reporting in the wracked condition of Zaire is more than can be expected.[8]

It is not difficult to see how the confrontation between different sectors of the world, which has been increasing in ferocity during the 1970s, has come to centre on the ways and the forms in which information passes through these many agencies and into the newspapers, radio and television stations of the world. At a very simple level, the arguments are between West and East and between North and South, but there are also many shadings of view and many views which have softened or hardened during the years in which the arguments have taken place. Indeed, almost all the participants would agree that certain improvements have already taken place in a very practical, non-ideological manner. In fact, statements made in the late 1970s by executives of the major agencies reveal a considerable shift of position and of understanding, compared with statements by individuals in similar positions five years before. Roger Tatarian, formerly Vice President of UPI, declared at a Cairo meeting in 1978:

> There is in fact imbalance in the flow of news, both in content and volume, from the developed to the developing world. . . . It is true that this reflects the disposition of global military, economic and political power. . . . Agency coverage often tends to seek simplistic solutions or Cold War ramifications in situations that are typically Asian, African or Latin American. . . . There is an acknowledged tendency among Western media . . . to devote the greatest attention to the Third World in times of disaster, crisis and confrontation. The agencies are no less interested in disaster, crisis and confrontation when it exists in the developed world. But their daily file of news of the developed world is vast, even when there is no crisis. The same is not true of much of the Third World.[9]

That really represents the present moderate view of the position, although it tends to be the two more distinct sides of the question that are more often heard.

The critics who range from Third World statesmen to academics such as Herbert Schiller[10] in the United States and Jeremy Tunstall[11] in England and Kaarle Nordenstreng[12] in Finland present a case to the effect that: the international news media are dominated by the four Western agencies which are imperialist in their nature; the image of the world which they offer is unbalanced by reason of their structure, history and professional intention, even though they are wedded in theory to doctrines of impartiality and accuracy. The agencies for their part argue that they provide reliable and comprehensive services to clients who are highly diverse in political, cultural and economic background; they assert that the accusations made against them tend to be put not really to create a better balance but simply to divert attention from illiberal and obscurantist domestic press policies in the complaining countries.

Very soon after the initiation of the debate a cry went up for empirical studies which would give the lie once and for all to one contention or the other. The empirical studies have followed, based on such data as the annual flow of television programmes around the world and the analysis of the content of agencies, word by word, story by story, over given periods of time. It would be otiose to plough through any of these in detail, for they have been produced by both sides and they suffer from the near impossibility of categorizing stories in a generally acceptable manner. It is very difficult to measure quantities of stories about 'disasters', for instance, and even harder to decide whether a given story is 'favourable' or not to a statesman or nation. Phil Harris, of the Leicester University Mass Communication Research Centre, undertook a study on behalf of UNESCO based on a review of 4,139 stories sent out in the course of one month by Reuters, AFP and UPI, broken down into regions and subject areas (see Tables 4 and 5). Harris, unlike many of the agencies' critics, concluded that they did not in fact transmit a noticeably pronounced picture of tragedy and disaster as endemic in the Third World, but that the Third World was rather presented in sketchy form and from ethnocentric perspectives in the process of satisfying a Western-dominated news market. Yet no one, on either side of the debate, has really felt convinced by the statistics which have been offered. Conferences of experts continue to propose further 'in depth' content analysis of agency output.

The centre of the problem is really the definition of news itself. We have seen a little of how the agencies have followed the information demands of their client media, originally for business information, later extending to material suitable for the popular press. The average Western reporter, trained in London or Paris or New York, would probably argue or at least feel that an item of news had to be

Table 3: Topic Coverage of Three Major Agencies

REGION	REUTERS No.	per cent	AFP No.	per cent	UPI No.	per cent
Western Europe	705	40·9	540	38·7	99	9·6
Northern America	241	14·0	155	11·1	727	71·2
Australia/New Zealand	32	1·9	9	0·7	1	0·1
The Levant	42	2·4	20	1·4	3	0·3
Middle East	141	8·2	107	7·7	31	3·0
USSR/Eastern Europe	70	4·1	49	3·5	15	1·5
Africa	160	9·3	184	13·2	18	1·8
Latin America	87	5·0	71	5·1	33	3·2
Indian sub continent	92	5·3	38	2·7	16	1·6
Far East	38	2·2	109	7·8	18	1·8
Asia	70	4·1	79	5·7	26	2·5
Other	44	2·6	33	2·4	35	3·4
	1722	100·0	1394	100·0	1022	100·0

Table 4: A Thematic Analysis of Five Major Subject Areas

REUTERS Story type	No.	per cent	AFP Story type	No.	per cent	UPI Story type	No.	per cent
Politics: Foreign	483	22·6	Politics: Foreign	446	25·7	Crime	248	19·5
Politics: Domestic	426	19·9	Sport	295	17·1	Politics: Domestic	202	15·9
Crime	300	14·1	Politics: Domestic	220	12·7	Economics: Domestic	190	14·9
Sport	229	10·7	Economics: Foreign	164	9·5	Politics: Foreign	128	10·0
Military	156	7·3	Crime	152	8·8	Human Interest	124	9·8

collected with care and had to be part of a comprehensive treatment of a subject, but that it would probably be of an unusual or exceptional nature in order to be 'newsworthy'. During the 1960s, the whole culture of journalism and the content of journalism education has been transformed with the arrival of the 'new journalism' of the underground and alternative press of the West and the 'investigative' journalism of the post-Watergate era. The Western journalist has come to see his role more as a kind of institutionalized permanent opposition, always looking critically askance at the doings of all those who hold official positions of power.

In certain ways, these developments in Western journalism have reaffirmed the oldest traditions of the craft, in that they hold up the pursuit of misdeeds as the highest ideal of reporting. Within the West itself, these reporting techniques and ideologies have been assailed on a number of grounds: firstly, there is a view that the very formula 'news story' rests on a set of social and political assumptions which are built into the judgements of newsworthiness and hidden inside the ideal of objectivity; secondly, there is an argument that the conflict which lies at the heart of the idea of a story automatically favours existing structures of power because these have become inured to the reporting system of Western society and feed it with the fodder it has come to require; thirdly, there is a case frequently made that the organization of news-gathering is an intrinsic element in a society's construction of reality or the image of reality—objectivity is merely that form in which information appears after it has passed through the professional procedures of journalism.[13] One researcher has argued, in fact, that objectivity is a defence rather than a practice, a 'strategic ritual' on the part of reporters.[14]

The researchers and journalists who have come to the defence of the Third World position have argued that developing societies have totally different requirements of their news media from the more prosperous and stable societies. News should not necessarily be conceived merely as a series of distinct events, but should be brought back always to a fundamental process. Where famine or riot are events, the problems of food production and agriculture, of excess population, of joblessness, are processes which need to be described before 'events' can be understood. A country may have struggled for decades to raise the money to build protection against flooding, with little attention being paid to it in the influential journals of the West; a major flood, however, will bring an army of reporters to peer at the homeless and criticize the way in which the relief programme is being administered on the ground. The argument is not one for good news rather than bad news, but for news in its due context. As one Indian journalist puts it: 'In our environment there is, and there will be for a long time to come, much that is ugly and distasteful. If we follow the Western norm we will be playing up only these dark spots and thus helping unwittingly to erode the faith and confidence without which growth and development are impossible.'[15] In other words, it is unfair or impossible to use, in the context of developing countries, a yardstick of newsworthiness which is not related to the problem of development. There may be objective news, but only within the confines of a set of news values, and these will vary according to the needs of a society. A journalist would have to share the commitment to the ideology of development before he would *see* the objective story in a developing society.[16]

Some Third World spokesmen would take this argument a stage further: the West refuses to concede the real case for development and interferes with the process instead of helping it; Western news agencies are not—as they constantly proclaim—answerable to their own societies, nor are they accountable to any other body or institution. They roam the world applying their standards and criteria freely to societies to which they have no commitment and from which their training has obliged them to be detached. They have become dangerous, in effect; their objectivity is, at best, unanchored, at worst, applied according to hostile formulae. This is why, in the cause of creating some kind of enforced accountability for the Western media, the Third World is demanding the creation of a New International Information Order.

There are variations of the argument. It has a certain cogency, though it is often deployed in the interests of authoritarian governments. Indeed, it is only a continuation of the argument which has been repeatedly made since the last decade when serious international debate started up concerning the presentation of the case for a new economic order. A search took place for journalistic forms in which difficult economic information could be placed before the public of the West. It was clear from the start that there was a conflict between purposeful reporting and instruction; where the former was permissible within the canons of the press, the latter fell into a different category, difficult to insinuate into newspapers which are designed to be read for ten or twelve minutes by working people with their own daily living problems to face in the industrialized countries. In many cases, developing countries' leaders were re-

peatedly disappointed with the frequent inability of sympathetic
Western journalists either to comprehend, or to report compre-
hensively, or to get their material into their papers.

In the 1960s and later, a group of journalists came into existence
in all of the 'quality' newspapers of Europe, Japan and the United
States, who have acted as important brokers between the developing
world and the élite of the West, but the popular newspapers have
very seldom measured up to the task. The problem entailed in the
new analogous cause—the New International Information Order—
is that the same cadre of reporters are not always sympathetic;
indeed, they sometimes now feel they are the objects of the criticism
although they may have spent a decade or more specializing in
Third World news, sincerely trying to convey the problems of
development to their readers.

Much of the criticism which has been levelled at the reporting of
Third World events in the Western press confuses the responsibility
of the world agencies with that of the important group of influential
foreign correspondents. In many ways, these two sources of international reporting feed each other, but their journalistic outlooks
are different, though both necessarily subject to the more general
and deep-seated concepts, built into Western civilization. The
agencies, of course, on the whole accept the prevailing Western idea
that news arises from the exceptional rather than the commonplace;
but they do attempt to supply their clients with a large quantity of
'rounded' and 'non-exceptional' information about Third World
societies. They do not dwell obsessively upon the negative, upon
criticism of governmental and financial failure, upon the troubles of
a society. Foreign correspondents, however, are very often under
great pressure to cover stories which emphasize the exceptional,
partly because the agencies are there to support a more constant
general purview. The foreign correspondent only really gets his or
her chance to publish stories of major prominence in a paper when
revolution or major change is taking place in the observed society.
There are, of course, many exceptions to this, but these tend to arise
in the wake of major 'disaster' or 'exception' news. Editors of
newspapers become interested in the general conditions of a society
shortly after it has filled the headlines for some more dramatic
reason. The general economic progress of a country is more likely
to be thought to be of interest to readers after it has passed through a
famine or drought or sudden change of government. The effect of the
more balanced assessment is then, in a way, merely to reconfirm or

slightly modify the mental image of the society concerned created earlier by the major story. To see why spokesmen of the Third World have been so shrill in their denunciation of the Western press one must therefore see the essential interconnectedness of the different parts of the international news system and the way in which the totality is drawn towards reinforcing the assumptions which the main societies of readership hold about the 'observed' societies.

One Third World politician who has made an analysis of a particularly interesting news incident and its treatment by North American newspapers is Christopher Nascimento, an official of the government of Guyana, who has castigated the accounts which were written about the Jonestown massacre of 1978.[17] The specific charges and ripostes need not concern us here so much as the three general issues which he raises, which help to illustrate the way in which reporting in the North about the South incorporates willy-nilly the images provided by history. Firstly, the newspapers, magazines and broadcasting coverage of the tragedy were said to reveal very little interest in the country where it took place. There are references to social and economic conditions but no attempt to analyse and no attempt to notice the connection even between the presence of Jim Jones in the hinterland of Guyana with the struggle of that country for economic survival: Guyana had been seeking to populate and develop unused lands by whatever means it could—the group of Jones's followers appeared to be a group of 'economically disenfranchized Americans with willing and productive hands' and had been welcomed to the country as a possible way to help diversify its fragilely narrow and dependent economy. The media did not see that the story illustrated one aspect of Guyana's attempt to escape from its appalling problems; rather, they filled in the general background with the odd, occasionally inaccurate brushstroke: the country's population was said to be 'illiterate' (although it is in fact 85 per cent literate) and one reporter referred to the Guyanese as speaking 'pidgin' English and a 'patois' (although the Guyanese speak a rather pure strain of English in an accent of their own).

Secondly, the blame for the incident was placed upon the government of Guyana, as if the authorities of a poor Third World nation possess or could possess the investigative apparatus of an industrialized society which would equip them with the kind of knowledge which exists in the files of the FBI or the CIA. This is not to judge what the government of Guyana could or should have done, but to indicate that media tend to use terms such as 'government' as if they meant the same thing whenever they are used.

Thirdly, Nascimento draws attention to a characteristic of the Western media which he dislikes but which, in a different context, can be presented as a virtue rather than a vice. He speaks of the 'almost universal determination on the part of the editors to protect the reputation of their reporters rather than expose their readers to the other side'. The organization of a newspaper or radio or television news bureau is based upon unified management; the senior members of it are supposed to guide the more junior while protecting them against interference from outside—normally the interference of government or of powerful outside interests involved in a story. That characteristic of management is ineradicable and in the context of the press is an important element in the protection of its freedom. None the less, when charges of ethnocentrism are being made, the managerial structure automatically reinforces the solidarity of the group against ideas as well as pressures. The procedures of reporting are transferred from country to country, wherever the story exists, and with them the full (often reinforced) protection of the headquarters office. An aggrieved individual (or nation) has no recourse to real justice through withdrawal or correction since there is no 'objective' point of contact, unless the law of one society or the other has been coincidentally transgressed. Nascimento's complaints stand.

There exist plans—among the demands in the New International Information Order—for an international news council or press council, of the kind which exists within the borders of a number of countries. It is unlikely that such a body will ever in fact emerge and if it did it would, for the reasons which gave rise to the demand for its existence, not really be able to offer an 'objectivity' which would convince the journalists of the North and the officials of the South at the same time. We must come to accept that the distortions which arise from world history are not curable by the creation of minor bureaucracies, still less by governmental intrusion into the business of collecting information. Something can be done through discussion and education, though much has to wait until the central intellectual crisis is resolved through changes in the structure of world power.

Meanwhile, politicians, administrators and journalists belonging to Third World countries continue to be infuriated and perplexed at the Western treatment of their problems and at the importation of the automatic reflexes of Western journalism. For instance, when a coup took place in Afghanistan in 1978, almost all informed Western newspapers treated the event as the occasion to inquire, 'Is the new leadership pro-West or pro-Soviet?' long before they came round to writing about conditions in Afghanistan or the importance of the new regime for its people. Very often when violent revolts or coups or counter-coups take place in African countries, the newspapers of the United States and Europe decide to focus on massacres of whites before they recount the slaughter of blacks. Yet Africa is a significant market for agency news as well as a source of information, and the news is flashed around the continent in the same form in which it reaches Europe; the inbuilt ethnocentrism of reporters working with their white European domestic audiences in mind is the phenomenon which arouses the anger of indigenous journalists, even sometimes those who have themselves been trained in the West.

The complaints of today are extraordinarily similar to those made in the United States in the early years of the century against the domination of the American news market by Reuters. 'So Reuters decided what news was to be sent from America. It told the world about the Indians on the war path in the West, lynchings in the South and bizarre crimes in the North. The charge for decades was that nothing creditable to America ever was sent,' writes Kent Cooper, General Manager of Associated Press.[18] At the conclusion of the First World War, the Director of *La Nacion* of Buenos Aires wrote to AP asking for it to extend its services to South America and abolish the Havas monopoly and declared: 'It is on the treatment accorded its press, however, that any given nation may see the true reflection of the respect it merits from any other nation. It almost goes without saying that both Brazil and Argentina were long considered conquered land so far as the Havas Agency propaganda purposes were concerned.'[19] Associated Press became the saviour of the reputations of nations in Asia and South America by driving out the European alliance of agencies; today it faces charges very similar to the ones it made itself in the early decades of the century.

There is, however, an important difference in the sheer quantity of material which circulates today and in the consequent greater relative power of editors over what is retailed to the readers. The present argument is much harder to unravel than in 1918, since the vicious circle of popular readers' tastes, editors' judgements and agency copy is more tightly drawn now than then. It is easy to make and repeat the basic charges, as, for example, Narinder Aggarwala, of the UN Development Programme, does in one widely quoted article,[20] but quite another to change the practice of Western journalism without impeding the freedom of Western journalists:

> The media, particularly the news agencies, will have to cure, at least partially, their all-pervasive obsession with so-called action or spot news, and not with soft or development news—economic and social development. Disasters, famines, corruption, wars, political intrigues, and civil disorders do make for action-packed and sexy copy while economic and social development is a very slow and, over short periods, an almost imperceptible process.

The perception gap between the journalism of exception and the journalism of development has perhaps never been better illuminated than during the convulsion in Iran leading to the collapse of the Shah. The failure of journalism which occurred in Iran during 1977 and 1978 can be blamed collectively on national and international agencies, resident international correspondents and visiting 'firemen' sent in by networks and newspapers; but it really highlights the way in which international reporting merely reflects the mutual images of different civilizations. A great upheaval, such as that in Iran, itself transforms those images; it changes the agenda of issues, as perceived in one society or another and thus changes the labels which are applied by journalists to new and old phenomena. Freedom fighters, for example, turn into religious extremists, terrorists into insurgents, etc., etc., all depending on the perspective of the reporter. The reaction of the Iranian masses to years of repression, when an opportunity to react turned up, was treated as the manipulated theatrical politics of Marxist opportunists in league with medieval zealots. The *Los Angeles Times* provided a good example of how the story was told very widely. 'Much of the recent rioting has grown from demonstrations called by religious extremists opposed to the Shah's attempt to Westernize this oil-rich, anti-Communist nation and to loosen the traditionally firm grip of the Moslem clergy.'[21] It was essentially the same line as that pursued—to their cost—by the diplomatic services of the principal Western countries involved in Iran. The media throughout the period during which the Shah's regime was cracking continued to give the impression that the Pahlavi dynasty was the only available 'sane' administration. Scarcely any report considered the ways in which the Shah's regime may have rendered itself progressively unacceptable to the people of the country. No report until well after the departure of the Shah started to analyse the real basis for the Ayatollah Khomeini's popularity; he was not treated with the credibility of, say, the

opposition leader of a Western country, at any time until his arrival
in power. The British press took to analysing the collapse of the
Shah in terms of the number of jobs lost in Britain, the contracts
lost to British and American companies, in ignoring the problems
suffered by the inhabitants of Iran.[22] This would not matter were it
not for the fact that the reports which appear in the principal newspapers of Britain and America circulate very far afield and are part
of an information complex which dominates the world, including
the Islamic countries, with a very different perspective on the eclipse
of the Shah.

An account of American newspapers' treatment of Iran was
provided by two writers in the *Columbia Journalism Review*[23] which
shows how many features of the reporting of Iran were systematic
reinterpretations rather than objective summaries. For example,
readers in the West were constantly told about a 'land reform' conducted by the Shah, which was resisted by the larger landowners.
True. But it was not made clear that the reform was conducted in
such a way as to spread the Shah's influence politically and diminish
the power of the landowners rather than bring about an agricultural
revolution. No major change in land-holding occurred, many
peasant families were forced to quit their holdings and move to the
overcrowded cities and Iran was obliged to import 50 per cent of her
food where previously she had been self-supporting. Yet the land
reform was one of the main examples frequently provided by reporters of the Shah's attempt to 'modernize'. It was not a question
of factual inaccuracy but of perspective; in the case of Iran the
contrast of perspective was total enough and the later refutation
dramatic enough for the pre-revolution reporting to be seen as
systematic distortion. The press of the West willingly accepted the
Shah's label of 'modernization'; in fact, however, there were more
unpleasant processes taking place: gross distortion of the distribution
of wealth, agriculture left without investment, enormous sums spent
on arms and on a series of cosmetic 'modern' projects, many of
which proved to be highly lucrative for Western consultants and
advisers. Very few newspapers really explained to their readers that
widespread opposition was developing during the last years of the
Shah's rule. *Time* magazine, for example, as quoted in *Columbia
Journalism Review*, wrote as late as 5 June 1978, after many thousands
had been killed in riots (enough to shake the credibility of a regime
in the eyes of the press reporting any African, Asian or South American country), that, 'The Shah also has a broad base of popular sup-

port, particularly in the army and among farmers and a newly created industrial working class, who have benefited from land reforms.'

The more sensational reporting (and therefore the more sensational the errors of perspective) tended to occur in magazines and in the reports of journalists who briefed themselves only from the narrow base of material available in newspaper files. However, agency reports tended to pursue the same line of thinking—a fundamentally Western line, emphasizing and re-emphasizing the binary mode of 'modernization' versus 'reactionary, religious bigotry'. AP, for instance, reported late in 1978:

> The source of the current turmoil is Iran's rush into the twentieth century, engineered by the Shah over the past fifteen years. In 1963, a decade after the United States helped him seize power, he began his effort to bring Iran's feudalistic society into the modern world. . . . But modernization has collided with ancient social and religious traditions, whose proponents refused to budge.[24]

It is difficult to go back over the reporting of Iran after two or three years without asking whether it reveals a major flaw in the whole system by which the public of the Western democracies is informed about the world.

One does not have even to accept the general argument of those who criticize the system of Western journalism and complain of the economic damage it does to the development of Third World countries to feel that all is not well with the lines of communication which pass through London, Paris and New York, nor with the procedures by which even admired and prominent Western reporters inform themselves about major events. It is easy to see how the ideology of Soviet reporters stands in the way of their collecting and presenting accurate information about the West; it is equally important for Western journalism to realize how deep may be their own ingrained ideological prejudices which act to the detriment of their own professional performance. To readjust the procedures of journalism to the actual reporting needs of the late twentieth-century world will be difficult. It has been made more difficult by the stubborn refusal of many institutions, corporations and individuals involved in the journalism of North America and Europe to accept that a critical problem exists and by the tendency of researchers, officials and journalists of many developing countries to exaggerate its consequences. Juan Somavia, of the Latin American Institute for Transnational Studies in Mexico, argues that the present system is 'a vehicle for transmitting values and life-styles to Third World countries which stimulates the type of consumption and the type of society necessary to the transnational expansion of capital'.[25] That goes too far. There do exist individual responsibilities and duties as well as forces of history. Journalism is an imperfect sub-system of an imperfect system but journalists have to act as if the former, at least, can be improved through effort.

The Managing Director of Reuters, Gerald Long, argues that the prevailing doctrine of journalism throughout the world is a journalism of exception, but that the interests of readers, within the market-oriented news, has none the less broadened considerably in recent years.

> A lot of us are not very satisfied with that criterion [the journalism of exception] as it operates in our societies, and obviously it won't be any more satisfactory as it operates internationally, but for better or worse that is the sort of journalism we practise. I think that the definition of news has broadened enormously—that vastly more people are interested, for example, in economic news than ten years ago. So the base of national and international news has broadened.[26]

Among Third World journalists there are those, like Tarzie Vittachi, who argue (as he did at a conference of the IPI in Australia in 1978) that news can be conceived as a combination of events and processes, without scrapping the 'free choice' relationship between editor and reader.

The question is whether indeed a determined effort by a news organization committed to development as a cause could actually shift the present categories of what material is wanted and what isn't. It is already known that the average metropolitan American newspaper publishes about a tenth of the material it collects each day in its computers from agencies and from its own staff. Even the enormous *New York Times* prints only about one-sixth of what it receives. With television the problem of time is even more acute. It is, furthermore, notoriously difficult to collect detailed information in many Third World countries; journalists have been subject to indiscriminate imprisonment, harassment, even assassination. Political pressure and implicit censorship have been increasing in many developing societies, and it is probable that an increased supply of Third World material would merely add to the unused quantity in the files of newspapers and magazines. However, several attempts have been made to create another 'new' journalism, or at least a new supply of information designed to encourage Western editors to see the point behind the Third World case. One of these is the Non-Aligned News Pool itself and the other is Inter Press Service.

Inter Press Service dates back to 1964, when it was started by a group of individuals belonging to South American states which had turned away from the path of social and economic reform. It emerged from a meeting held in Germany of Latin American and European journalists who had been associated with an organization called the Roman Press Agency, which had mainly dealt in feature material concerning Latin American development issues. Those attending the German meeting became the shareholders of the new IPS and although IPS continues to operate as an international non-profit co-operative with its headquarters in Buenos Aires, nearly all of the original shareholders have left, after the political reorientations of the last decade.

The news service decided to dedicate itself to the presentation of material dealing with the problems of South America but also of the Third World in general (it has very strong links with some of the revolutionary forces in newly liberated states in Africa), and to do so within a broad interpretative framework. Its material is sent to unions, companies, universities, religious groups, as well as to publications. In its early days it saw its role as that of forging a link of understanding between South American countries and Europe, in order to encourage projects of economic reform which had some appeal in both continents. As the political situation in South America changed, however, and The Alliance for Progress born of J. F. Kennedy's idealism faded away, that became increasingly difficult and IPS had to withdraw from many countries. In the 1970s it changed tack and became a specialized news agency, its colours clearly nailed to the mast of decolonization and development. Whereas in the early days it had simply taken governmental material from Peru, Argentina, Chile and sent it out cheaply by radio tele-printer (in exchange for payment from those governments), it gradually became disillusioned with the possibility of creating a mood of reform while depending upon official patronage. Many of the South American governments with whom IPS was doing business cancelled their contracts and IPS managed to conclude an agreement with Tanjug whereby its material was circulated around the world but credited to the Yugoslav agency. Later, similar co-operative arrangements were made with the Iraqi, Venezuelan and Libyan agencies. Various UN agencies and special conferences took official note of IPS's existence. In 1964, the non-aligned movement was itself young and inexperienced and IPS has gathered great strength from the greatly enhanced political prestige of the movement among Third World nations in the 1970s.

IPS's material is current but is informed by a desire to keep its clients up-to-date on a series of permanent issues: e.g., relations between Third World and industrial countries, the ways in which they co-operate among themselves to overcome domination, and examination of the policies of the major powers towards the developing world. But it is important not only because it is a professional body which has rejected all the traditional Western journalistic precepts and espoused a specific political cause without apology. It has also attempted to translate the problems of one section of the globe into an entirely new journalistic practice.

IPS is non-hierarchic in its internal management arrangements; links are offered to all Third World agencies to become partners via the co-operating journalists in IPS. It sees its function as that of co-ordinating an alliance against continuing imperialism and its basic target audience is therefore the Third World itself which, because of the paucity of existing communication facilities, is not entirely aware of its own predicament. The audience in the developed world is also within its range but it seeks to present itself to this public as an alternative to their present sources of information; it seeks to move them beyond mere social concern towards an active understanding of the problems of dependence. Its whole emphasis is therefore away from the 'spot' news of existing news agencies, towards analysis and narrative. Its journalists argue that the traditional agencies operate within a news market which has created a need for isolated nuggets of information which systematically deprive their readers of the kinds of understanding which IPS wishes to encourage. It is, in a sense, trying to do within its own context what many news-reformers within the West have argued should be done with Western radio and television news—exploit the non-transactional nature of the broadcast audience by making news deliberately educative and interpretative. Peter Jay, formerly British Ambassador in Washington, and his television colleague, John Birt, have long been advocates through the London *Times* of this kind of reform within broadcast journalism in Britain and have attached to the argument the tags 'bias against understanding' (which is allegedly built into the existing system) and 'issue journalism' (which is the desired solution). The Western parallels are only partial. IPS operates within a political line which attracts principally the intelligentsia of the Third World whom it seeks to co-opt.

In its decade and a half of existence, IPS has acquired an immense network of contacts and expertise. It has satellite circuits linking Buenos Aires with a series of Latin American bureaux in sixteen countries. A bureau in Rome acts as co-ordinator for messages passing through the Middle East, Africa and Asia. Altogether, 200 journalists are employed, working either alone or within the bureaux. Apart from its daily bulletin of information and a daily teleprinter service of feature material, IPS serves a large number of weekly publications with a number of detailed regular surveys; there is a weekly strategic survey of Latin America, for instance, analysing issues relating to armaments, and parallel agricultural and economic surveys. It prepares a mining survey and a weekly oil bulletin, analysing the activities of the oil companies operating in the region. Every week, too, there is produced a bulletin on the activities of sympathetic groups working in the Catholic Church in Latin America, reporting on their relationships with the relevant regimes. In its dealings with the national agencies with whom it has contacts it agrees to act as transmitter rather than editor; it has agreed to send out material from these agencies without altering a word of the copy, appending their rather than its byline. In some cases it will incorporate the national agency's material into its own and append a double byline. As the Non-Aligned News Pool has gradually established its service, the work of IPS has developed as collaborating supplement.

The News Pool was brought into existence by a decision of the Fifth Non-Aligned Summit Conference in Colombo of August 1976, by which eighty-five nations decided to share information from their respective agencies in order to 'achieve the broad and free circulation among themselves of news, information, reports, features and photographs about each other, and also provide objective and authentic information relating to non-aligned countries and to the rest of the world'.[27] Their intention was, in the words of the political declaration which accompanies the plan, to overcome 'the situation of dependence and domination in which the majority of countries are reduced to being passive recipients of biased, inadequate and distorted information'.[28] It is possible to wonder about the sincerity of this declaration, since in developing countries outside Latin America it is only the rare national agency which actually permits a flow of news from the much disliked international news agencies direct to the newspapers or radio stations of the country; the whole flow of news from outside is vetted by government agencies for any damaging references to itself in three-quarters of the countries concerned. The agencies are there to carry out the collection rather than the sale of information; indeed, in many cases the collection of information is also very closely supervised by government officials. The flow of news passes into government rather than the press and is used to keep politicians and bureaucracy aware of what is happening in other parts of the world. The decision to form the Non-Aligned News Pool was, therefore, more an act of political solidarity than a pragmatic decision. Governments would continue taking the material of the big agencies—even if they continued to denounce their bias, partiality, triviality and distortion. Newspapers would not be permitted to disturb their readers with their material. However, through the News Pool the nations concerned might acquire greater leverage over the way in which their own image is presented to the world.

In 1975, Tanjug had already started the Tanjug Pool, from which the Non-Aligned News Pool grew. Participating agencies at first sent their material to Tanjug by any means at their disposal (including IPS) with a limit of 500 words per day. Tanjug also monitored the output of certain agencies and made a selection of material. Forty-one agencies are now regular participants of the News Pool, but the majority of material is in practice contributed by about seven countries, of which Yugoslavia herself is the most active. Very little of the material is critical of nations or political positions, although a large amount of it is ideological and polemical. One research project which has analysed the output over a period found little overt bias against the United States in the reports which were issued and only a few stories were hostile to the American government or interests—far less than in the output of an international agency. The News Pool was not conceived as a supranational agency of the non-aligned countries—it was intended to reinforce their unity, as Pero Ivacic, Director General of Tanjug, puts it.[29] Tanjug translates and disseminates its selection of material in French, English and Spanish and by December 1977 was sending out up to forty items a day, with the volume slowly increasing.

Today the structure has broadened out; of the redistribution centres, five have been made regional centres, at which material is received, slightly edited, translated and retransmitted. A great deal of the material at first received was clearly unsuitable for publication in any newspaper hoping to hold the attention of its readers, but the mere existence of the News Pool and the fact that its selection of material does actually reach a large number of newsrooms has slowly helped to train news agencies in a number of countries to search their societies for more appropriate information. Tanjug clearly sees its task as that of silent tutor, patiently coaxing many of the agencies in alliance with it to adopt a journalistically realistic attitude to the task. Some of the agencies have never attempted to do anything in the past other than hand out turgid speeches by their heads of state and unhelpful (even sometimes unreliable) statistical public-relations material. The News Pool might, by improving the flow of material which emanates from Third World national agencies, help to bridge the gap, but there are clear limits to its future possible achievements. Countries in which all information is closely controlled by government cannot, by definition, sacrifice their sovereignty over that information to an agency located outside their borders.

The intensity of the debate over the role of the world agencies which raged during the months while UNESCO was reaching its compromise Declaration on the Mass Media in November 1978 has somewhat abated. Both sides are perhaps trying to see whether any damage has been sustained or inflicted. On the one hand, the complaining governments of the Third World have been tarred as hypocrites, practising censorship and harassment at home while denouncing distortion and bias abroad. On the other the agencies have been made to look insensitive to the real problems and the real indignation which has motivated at least some of the criticism. UNESCO has called for 'balance' in the flow of news without reducing the commitment to 'free flow' of news. That appears to be sheer humbug to the supporters of the Western position, since balance can only be guaranteed through intervention while freedom can only be secured without it. None the less, there is a feeling that the argument over the agencies has now moved one step towards the practical and one step away from the purely polemical. The moderate tones of the Report of the Twentieth Century Fund Task Force on the International Flow of News are a good example of the tendency of Western opinion.

Fundamentally, as has been argued from the start, the inequalities between sectors of the globe are the result of the colonial past and a product of the historical circumstances which make up the world as it is. The news agencies have emerged from that history, as have all

Table 5: Figures Relating to Some Internationally Active Agencies

Press Agency	Number of countries served	Number of subscribers	Number of countries covered by correspondents and stringers	Number of words issued daily	Number of regular staff	Number of correspondents in foreign countries
AP (USA)	108	1,320 newspapers 3,400 broadcasters in USA 1,000 private subscribers	62 foreign bureaux	17 million		559
UPI (USA)	92	7,079 newspapers 2,246 clients outside USA + 36 national news agencies	81 foreign bureaux	11 million 200 news pictures	1,823	578
AFP (FRANCE)	152	12,000 newspapers 69 national agencies	167 countries 108 foreign bureaux	3,350,000 + 50 news pictures	1,990 incl.	171 full-time corres. 1,200 stringers
REUTERS (UK)	147	6,500 newspapers & 400 radio and TV stations	153 countries	1,500,000	2,000 incl.	350 full-time corres. 800 stringers
TASS (USSR)	80	13,000 subscribers 200 subscribers to Tass photo 325 foreign subscribers	110 countries 40 bureaux		professional staff 560	61 corres.
DPA (FRG)	78	144 foreign subscribers 55 film services	80 countries 37 film services	115,000	800 incl.	105 full-time corres.
ANSA (ITALY)	69	1,600 (circa)	69 bureaux	300,000	568 incl.	47 full-time corres. 295 stringers

EFE (SPAIN)	32	1,734	52	500,000	545	123
KYODO (JAPAN)	37	33 national agencies 40 foreign news agencies 64 Japanese newspapers 59 commercial radio and TV stations 14 non-member newspapers	37 bureaux	220,000 letters in Japanese 35,000 words in English	1,900	
TANJUG (YUGOSLAVIA)	103		46	75,000 to 120,000 news pictures + 40–50	896 incl.	46 full-time corres.
IPS INTER PRESS SERVICE	36	19 national agencies 400 newspapers, weeklies and institutions	50	100,000	390	44
MENA	25	13 national agencies for exchange of news 21 national agencies for exchange of photos	35	185,000 200 documentary films 200 news pictures	500 incl.	35 full-time corres.

Source: The World of News Agencies Working Paper No. 11 of the UNESCO Commission for the Study of Communication Problems.

the institutions and beliefs of the West. The major income of the agencies comes from the wealthier nations and while the picture of the world compiled daily by these agencies is intended to be systematic and coherent, it is so in the light of the clients' needs and interests, and these are *Western*. The whole technical structure of the agencies, their economic interest and their professional alignment is towards the West, even though the developing nations continue to derive most of their information about the world from the same world agencies. There is nothing that the Non-Aligned News Pool, or IPS or the many other small well-meaning organizations specializing in Third World news can do to overcome the preponderance of AP, UPI, AFP and Reuters.

The problem really lies outside the control of the agencies, in the West's pre-existing image of the developing world built of its own frustrated hopes, and the selfishness and paternalism of history. It is what the agencies and Western journalism as a whole do *inadvertently* which is the trouble. We do not get an image of the United States or France or Germany as consisting only of murders and fires and terrorists, because those countries are constantly creating knowledge of themselves through their physical and cultural exports, through the work of their own journalism, through the reporting done within their own borders by reporters from all over the world. The Third World does not benefit from the same profusion of sources. It impinges on Western consciousness in disproportionately negative ways. We think of the price of motor cars as necessarily rising, through no one's fault; we think of the price of petrol rising as a direct result of the 'greed' of a few Arabs. There lies the root cause of the imbalance, and journalism alone can do little to restore it. Journalists, however, could train themselves to be sensitive to the phenomena of what one might call conceptual imbalance, moral unfairness, the application of uniform standards where they cannot be appropriate.

Our mental media picture of the world is compounded of our Western interests within it and is supportive therefore of those interests. The struggle to escape from our bad image of the Third World is an essential stage in *its* struggle for independence. In this sense the journalism of the West is helping to arrest the historic process of development, and if there is any point at which the vicious circle of dependence can be broken, it is there, in the intractable issue of information, though it may take a leap of imagination among journalists to achieve it.

4. And a New International Electronic Order?

In the last ten to twenty years we have come to use the word 'information' in different ways from the past and the very broadening of the use of the term in the debate about the international flow of information is intimately connected with the development of modern electronics. In the era of the computer, information has come to be seen as the raw material which, when reduced to the dot-and-dash binary codes which computers use, can be bought and sold as a commodity itself. In one sense, news agencies have always bought and sold information for media and business use, but in the age of the computer a far greater range of material has been processed for storage in computers and transmission between them. The great telecommunication highways which distribute information within nations and between nations have displaced transportation highways as the core communication systems of a modern society—and of the modern world. If all the banks shut their doors but maintained their telecommunication links it would still be possible for a monetary economy to continue in existence. If the production plants of all the newspapers in the world suddenly ceased it would be possible to transmit (certainly through the developed countries) sufficient knowledge about economic, agricultural, military, diplomatic and cultural affairs for society to continue much the same.

The latest developments in telecommunications make it possible for all the internal mail of major companies, all of the content of radio and television stations, all the material which passes into newspapers, all of the monetary transactions between large organizations and within them, all of the new sensing devices which analyse weather, harvests, troop movements and mineral deposits, to be conducted electronically rather than by normal physical means. Indeed, it is thought that in time it will even be possible to transmit energy from space through the electro-magnetic spectrum. Energy itself will have been reduced to the condition of information.

The Japanese were the first to apply the tag Information Society to this stage in the growth of the industrial era and a host of sociologists, researchers, visionaries and prophets have been at work for a decade analysing the political, geo-political, psychological, religious and moral implications of this great transformation. It is a transformation of perception as much as of reality, for society has of course always been based upon information. But until the coming of modern electronics, we did not think of class relationships, government, economics and diplomacy as if they were mere functions of information transfer. In fact, they are not, but they can be very usefully visualized as if they were, and this is why the information debate between developed and developing nations has invaded the whole sphere of information economics. For the world distribution of the means of production and distribution of information is grossly unequal and part of the quest for a New International Information Order consists in an attempt to redress this aspect of information inequality.

Information is a very different kind of commodity from any other, even though it has come to be treated in many respects as if it were merely another manufactured good. For one thing, information constantly acquires additional usefulness as it passes through the manufacturing process: it can pass through books and magazines, libraries and education systems, business houses and mail systems. A piece of information acquired from an ancient manuscript may pass into a learned paper, then into a biography, then into the treatment for a television programme, then a cinema film and end up on a videodisc or video-cassette. At every stage, its legal status will be different; different departments of government may be concerned with it, different business men may profit from it, but it need never cease to circulate to somebody's entertainment, interest or profit. The same nugget of information may cause scholars to argue and dispute, novelists and psychoanalysts to ponder implications, seamstresses and scene-builders and make-up artists to formulate plans, plastic manufacturers to produce tapes and discs. Information is also implicit in command functions and may substitute for layers of human management in a complex factory process which can only operate correctly when data concerning markets and public demand is co-ordinated with data concerning supplies and data from the different sections of the same plant. At each point information is the linkage between states; it is a kind of raw material itself which is contained within the product whose manufacture has depended upon it. Manufactured goods are in many senses frozen information.

It is very likely that in years to come an information ring main system will be used in homes and offices rather like the electricity ring main system of today. A single circuit could supply all of the information modes which a household of the present or the future could require: electronic mail, radio and television entertainment, a personal selection of audio-visual programmes from a library store, the contents of a book, the records of a firm's book-keeping, the files for calculating wages and the command system for paying them. One can already see the crude prototypes for this 'domestication' of high-capacity information in some of the new national videotex systems—such as Captains in Japan, Telidon in Canada, Qube in Ohio, Prestel in Britain and Antiope in France. They are primitive versions of what may one day emerge—mass terminal systems, connected to large public databases and larger private information stores to supply the individual home with a huge variety of services.

For the purposes of our argument, it is the concept behind these rather than any judgement of their existing quality which matters. The distinctions which could come about between societies well endowed with such systems and societies without them could be much greater than any distinctions in income indices separating societies today. It is bad enough to have an appalling telephone network in a world where wealthy countries have good, sufficient and well-maintained telephone circuits. It would be much worse to undertake the task of economic development in a world in which the major manufacturing powers supplement physical energy with sophisticated information systems which constantly enhance the disparities between themselves and the less developed societies. The deprived society would recede further and further into the status of object rather than subject. It would be more helplessly locked inside the spiral of low-information generation than today. Its élite would be drawn into the appreciation of the developed world's high-level provision, causing further disfiguration of the former society's patterns of entertainment, education, social status and reward. The divisions between the information-rich and the information-poor—internationally and nationally—could become almost inexorable, far harder to overcome than the divisions founded upon economic exploitation. Information wealth is difficult to sequestrate or tax or render equitable once it has been acquired. As we see today within societies with socially demarcated education systems, information gaps create further gaps in wealth and social status. They are intangible but self-replicating.

It is possible to view information as a social resource of a special kind rather than as a produced commodity, a resource which enables other resources to function productively since it is the existence of salient information which determines the value and existence of other resources. Creating blockages in the flow of information is the technique of power within autocratic systems of government and these are generally in themselves hindrances to economic expansion. That is partly why the argument about 'free flow' is the modern counterpart of the more traditional argument about a free press: it is no longer possible to separate official attitudes to political censorship from the policy of a society towards its information flow as a whole. Information, when treated as a resource, raises automatically the wider question of social allocation and social control, since by its nature information arises from society, or a country, as a whole but has to be allocated to specific interests in order to be exploited. It is thus like a mineral resource. The problems of privacy, access, commercial privilege, public interest, are problems of allocation and priority and value of the kind that every society has had to debate incessantly in history and has now to do so again in this new guise. Computer science has created its own devices—encryption, coding, metering—by which the information flow may be diverted or made to circulate only within special groups or for specified purposes. The internationalization of the discussion about information thus raises many of the traditional questions in a new form.

Societies possess information rights, perhaps privacy and *non*-communication rights, as well as rights to provide and receive knowledge. National independence is more than ever dependent upon the ability to make local determinations concerning the handling of information; for example, a society with no access to satellite sensoring data about itself is unable to control its own economic destiny and can in no real sense any longer be thought to be 'free'. Yet that nation may not be able physically or economically to control the technology through which the information about itself travels and in which it is stored. That is why the problems arising from new conceptions of information are very complex and are inseparable from the whole bundle of issues which have been subjected to scrutiny under the New International Information Order. To comprehend the demands which are made under that rubric one has to recognize the altered nature of information, now that it has become possible to treat it as a national resource.

The newest technologies developed by half a dozen of the advanced nations enable the users to acquire, to hold and to retrieve more information more efficiently than in the past. Knowledge concerning resources in the ground, weather, market conditions or technology itself provides the nations and companies which have it with enormous advantages in the communications process. One may cite as an example the case of the World Administrative Radio Conference of 1979 held in Geneva at which the complex technical arguments over the organization of use of the electro-magnetic spectrum—radio wavelengths—was carried out. The American delegation had a staff in Geneva of more than a hundred, compared with one or two from some of the smallest countries; nearly a thousand people had been involved in preparing the US plans for this important general WARC; with the use of massive computer expertise the US had mapped out a negotiating position covering the entire spectrum from 1 hertz to 387 gigahertz with a complex set of fallback positions. The delegation had also collected all known facts concerning the positions of all other delegations as well as informal information collected in private briefings and everything relevant that could be found out about the members of all of the other delegations. The whole of this information could be held on-line and could be retrieved in a matter of moments. It provided the United States with a tremendous advantage over all of its rivals. The world power game has moved into an information phase.

The great majority of the information resources—both natural and industrial—are controlled by a tiny proportion of humanity. The fact that the electro-magnetic spectrum is a capacity of *nature* and is therefore the property of all has meant, however, that there *has* to be a certain level of international co-operation before anyone can exploit it. The 1950s were the years of the great arms build-up. Economies of East and West diverted an enormous share of investment and materials to an arms race which provided a longish period of relative political stability. The proportion of gross national product in the West which is devoted to arms has dropped from nearly 9 per cent to a little over 6 per cent during the 1970s, and it now seems that industrialized economies are in need of a major boost of activity. It seems possible that this will come from a massive build-up and re-equipping of societies with information devices. To realize the full potential of the information society will involve a rewiring of society, the laying down of new networks and the manufacturing of vast quantities of terminal equipment—from domestic robots to home facsimile and telemail machines. The effectiveness and rapidity with which simple devices like the pocket computer have moved from luxuries to universal necessities in a few years exemplify the way in which high-technology equipment can be cheapened and widely disseminated. The pocket calculator, however, is a positively crude and cumbersome device compared with what is now technically and industrially possible if political, investment and managerial decisions are co-ordinated. A kind of scramble for media is underway in the industrialized world, on a scale similar to the first arms race of the post-war era. It can bring employment and apparent stability to Western economies for many years. The developing world has already provided a number of inexpensive manufacturing branch economies in Korea, Taiwan, Hong Kong and many more will be needed if the total re-equipping of the world with information hardware comes to fruition in the mid-1980s. One important question, however, is whether this new stage in the evolution of already industrialized economies will increase still further the appalling inequalities between the developed and Third Worlds which have become a vexation of the 1960s and 1970s.

Those developing economies which have achieved, through nationalization or successful indigenous investment, an area of independently controlled economic growth now find themselves more urgently in need of information than in the past. The need for information is itself one of the consequences of independence. Outsider advice is not always as effective as expertise culled from the experience of indigenous management. It is extraordinarily difficult to leap onto the bandwagon of development; the sheer ability to exploit the information available from outside often depends upon the existence of various kinds of infrastructure—from schools and training colleges to computers and transportation—which may not be in place. The irony of the present situation of many of the developing nations is that they are painfully negotiating their way into an impasse, which may not be noticed until a later state in their growth. The adaptation to sophisticated forms of agriculture in parts of Asia is a good earlier parallel: countries adapted to 'miracle rice' and later found that the requirements for petroleum-based fertilizers after the 1973 oil crisis imposed a crippling burden of further dependence. Turning towards information equipment as an object of investment could itself lead in the next decade to further frustrations and multiplying inequalities if developing societies find themselves caught up in the information scramble without a real indigenous base of manufacture and expertise. Of course, there is also a powerful argument to the effect that the information stage of North and South economies is making both sides more mutually dependent than in the past; the industrialized countries can only acquire the necessary economies of scale by selling their equipment partly in Third World countries and often by storing data sensitive to themselves in places which happen to be in the developing world. None the less, even in a situation of interdependence, the more powerful and the more independent can use the relationship itself for improving their relative position. Better access to information acts like a lever, greatly multiplying the ability to exploit one's own resources.[1]

Yet despite this lugubrious prognosis, a series of real opportunities do exist at the start of the 1980s. Technological change in the information field means a dramatic decrease in the costs of microprocessors, of telecommunications systems and especially of access to satellites. Greater storage volume is available at lower cost. These facts in themselves ought to mean that societies which have perceived the way to use these technologies could find an inexpensive and rapid route to industrialization—always providing that the technology is transferred at a pace consistent with the development of indigenous expertise. It should be possible, for example, to bypass the traditional methods for establishing mass telephone and radio systems; it should be possible to develop an effective medium of advertising without the extremely expensive task of creating a multi-layered newspaper industry of the kind developed throughout the West in the late nineteenth century. What is certain is that only with the thoroughgoing provision of communication devices will a society be able to achieve the economic take-off so long predicted by development economists and so painfully deferred. What has to be avoided at all costs is a dumping of cheap hardware on a society which has not thought through the processes by which the need for it will be built up and exploited. In other words, it is through the acquisition of an autonomous perspective—an indigenous information control—that information equipment can become a tool and not a further burden.

II

It is in the light of this argument that one may examine that aspect of the New International Information Order which deals with the control and management of the electro-magnetic spectrum. This area of science and public policy is treated normally as a highly technical matter in which the layman, when he feels he has mastered the fundamental issues, is waved aside from the discussion by the attendant experts, while the skein of issues grows more tangled as it unravels itself. But the geo-political tensions behind the allocation of Hertzian waves to different uses are as political as they are technical and often even the most experienced telecommunications technicians find themselves unconsciously indulging in politics.

The spectrum is the resource upon which the exploitation of all information resources (or almost all) depends. It is based upon the facility which exists in nature (and which has been explored since the last years of the last century) by which electro-magnetic energy can be made to oscillate, to move in waves, at different rates; the spectrum itself consists of the total range of possible rates of oscillation. If you stand at a particular point and a long skipping-rope is waved before you there is a constant distance between the 'crest' of each wave; this is called the 'wavelength'. But since all electro-magnetic waves travel at the same speed—186,000 miles per second—the wave peaks and troughs will occur at a higher frequency the shorter the distance between them. The longer the wavelength the lower the frequency. One cycle per second is the basic unit of measurement known as one hertz; one thousand cycles is one kilohertz, one million is one megahertz and one thousand million one gigahertz. At the smallest end of the spectrum the waves cannot be heard or seen and for the purposes of radio communication the available frequencies range from 10 kilohertz to 300 gigahertz.

For eighty years now it has been possible for man to use more and more of the spectrum for sending information and entertainment, either from point to point or in broadcast mode to general audiences. Each information device which has been developed during the twentieth century uses up more of the available frequencies and careful international organization—through the International Telecommunication Union (ITU), the world's oldest international organization, dating back to 1865—is necessary to avoid the squandering of spectrum space. Unlike other international agencies, the ITU exists only through its members, who make unanimous decisions from decade to decade on how to govern the use of this flexible resource of nature. Different devices, from radio and television to computer data sent via satellite, utilize different quantities of spectrum, or different amounts of 'bandwidth': one colour television channel, for example, uses as much bandwidth as 2,000 ordinary telephone circuits or 40 FM radio channels. The members of the ITU have gradually over the decades divided the total spectrum into bands within which specific services may be transmitted: there are twenty of these in all, including radio and television broadcasting, radio astronomy, mobile radio, point to point communication, etc.

One further world resource is interconnected with the spectrum and that is the orbit around the globe at a distance of 22,000 miles within which satellites may be 'parked' in such a way as to enable three of them to send signals to the entire world. There are already many 'sets' of satellites of this kind, known as geo-stationary satellites because at their particular height they move at the same speed as the earth. Even in the few years since space communication became possible, so many satellites have been sent up to use that particular orbit around the earth that it is in danger of becoming cluttered. Only a handful of nations have hitherto acquired the expertise to launch satellites of their own and these and their client nations today require ever more parking spaces within this very convenient orbit.

The geo-stationary orbit and the electro-magnetic spectrum are both different from earth resources such as oil, coal or gas, in that they never run out. They are different from crops because no amount of effort on the part of mankind can increase them. In some ways they are comparable to water resources, in that mischievous or unco-operative exploitation can make them useless but they will always regenerate their usefulness if the mischief or excessive use is removed. There is a further way in which they can be 'stretched' which makes them comparable to water, in that skilful and economic use can multiply the benefits they offer.

A radio station of the 1920s would use three or four times as much bandwidth as a similar radio station of today; more advanced equipment at transmitter end and at receiving end has meant that the spectrum is less wasted than in the past. Each decade makes further economies possible, but always at a higher level of technology, so that nations with primitive transmitters can be branded as 'squanderers' of the spectrum. Nations which exceed the level of power which has been permitted them on a given bandwidth may destroy the signals of others. Spectrum warfare has often broken out on the frequencies which are most commonly used for long-distance radio messages and a number of stations have occupied the short waves with the intention of disseminating national propaganda across the world in signals powerful enough to render the band useless to others who have legitimate rights to it. In fact, on the short wave, anything up to a quarter of the users are guilty of one form of misbehaviour or another (in technical parlance, they are 'out of band'), so desirable and in such short supply are its frequencies.

It is important to point out, however, that in international terms 'short supply' has a different meaning from its use in relation to other resources. No nation has *ever* been refused permission to introduce any service requiring radio frequencies as a result of shortage. It has always been possible for telecommunications experts to find a suitable band and overcome overcrowding of the airwaves, because equipment is constantly becoming more sophisticated and less wasteful and because a combination of geography, technology and careful planning has always so far helped to compensate for inequalities between societies caused by the lateness at which the developing societies entered into the industries and services which use the spectrum.

In satellite communication, the allotment of a space in the orbit is not, however, sufficient to enter the business of communicating data; it is also necessary to have the right to use a frequency in the spectrum along which to send data up to the satellite and another frequency to transmit it back to the receiving station located at some suitable place on the globe. Satellites are also now being used for broadcasting purposes and, international regulations permitting, every nation sufficiently equipped will soon be able to reach its entire population (or that of another nation) without the trouble and expense of erecting hundreds or thousands of transmitters within line-of-sight of all of the television receivers in the land; it will be sufficient to transmit direct from a satellite either to hundreds of miniature ground stations or eventually direct to the domestic receivers. But this development, too, depends upon the distribution of appropriate satellite orbits and frequency spectrum space.

The ITU performs the increasingly complex and politically sensitive task of allocating bandwidths to services and registering each individual nation's frequency usage. Every few years there is held a World Administrative Radio Conference to allocate the whole of the spectrum to the new services which technology has thrown up in the meantime or to reallocate it to take account of improvements and economies in bandwidth which have become possible in existing services. The ITU also holds WARCs to sort out specific problems within specific areas of the spectrum, as well as more wide-ranging ones such as the WARC of late 1979 in Geneva which dealt with the reallocation to services of an immense part of the spectrum. As the information debate has progressed, the issue of spectrum allocation has become intensely politicized and arguments concerning a particular use of the short wave or a particular band within the gigahertz range have taken on the same kind of ideological coloration as arguments over oil resources or frontiers or coffee prices. However, despite differences in politics and ideology, the member nations of the ITU have succeeded in sharing the resources of the electro-magnetic spectrum without a tenth of the confusion which has broken out over control of other resources and commodities. This is not the place to unravel the often mindbendingly labyrinthine arguments which discussion of the spectrum can lead to, but merely to show how the controversy over information rights and the New International Information Order have irreversibly spilled into the arena of the ITU.[2]

The inequalities of provision in telecommunications are sometimes dramatically illustrated. During the Sadat-Begin talks in Cairo, the presidential jet of the United States brought a posse of aides to Egypt, one of whom needed urgently to speak to his colleagues in a downtown hotel. The hotel's interchange line was busy. He tried again. It was out of order. The aide, in exasperation, returned to the plane and set up a link via satellite from the tarmac at Cairo to Washington, D.C. and thence back again via satellite direct to the hotel—a distance of some tens of thousands of miles. President Sadat's aides could not have performed a comparable feat at Kennedy Airport (and would not have had to).

The incident illustrates the way in which advantages of scale in telecommunications breed further advantages of versatility. Of the 400 million telephones in existence around the world in 1978 only 30 million belonged to subscribers in Latin America, Africa and Asia combined, areas which contain three-quarters of the world's population. Yet the developed world is still adding telephones faster than this three-quarters and every additional telephone added to a network enhances the total usefulness of the network. Arithmetic additions to a network open up exponential increases in value, and the already dominant nations are bursting with plans for further networks, for data, voice and mobile links, for citizen band, and for direct broadcast satellites, which will multiply their ability to hold information wealth.

In the past it was sufficient for the ITU to ask the intending users of a section of the spectrum to form an orderly queue, as it were, and stake their claims. Today the demand from the developing countries is for the handing out of spectrum rights to nations who are far from being ready to exploit them. For example, the developing world was instrumental at the special WARC of 1977 in forcing the world to accept a general distribution of the frequencies which would be used for direct broadcast satellites; it will be decades before more than one or two of the developing nations have their own satellites and the United States argued fiercely—to the point of threatening to refuse to co-operate with the final arrangement, or in ITU parlance of 'entering a reservation'—for those nations now able to exploit satellites to be permitted free use of the frequencies according to traditional practice. The ITU has normally allowed a controlled form of 'squatters' rights' to prevail, so long as each nation registers its use with the International Frequency Registration Board, keeps each service within the appropriate section of the spectrum, and observes the rules of mutual non-interference. The developing world, however, has been adopting a deliberate policy of trying to restrict the technological advantages which accrue to countries which develop early the economic and industrial capacity to exploit a world resource. At the 1979 WARC they voted to have their own national frequencies allotted in the gigahertz range (for their non-existent satellites). There are powerful general arguments against 'squatting' and in favour of the temporary non-use of frequencies: America's Public Broadcasting System, for instance, only exists because of the foresight of the Federal Communications Commission (the domestic agency which regulates the use of the spectrum by American broadcasters as well as all industrial services which require frequencies) which refused to allow further television stations onto the popular VHF band in the late 1940s. For several years no further 'squatting' was allowed to domestic American commercial broadcasters on this band and fifteen years later the result was that, in a changing social climate, America was able to construct on UHF and VHF bands some hundreds of educational and public stations; these today provide the United States public with a national non-commercial broadcasting system on the popular VHF band. It could be said that the developing world is demanding a similar moratorium but on an international plane which could result in a cheap world communication system at the turn of the century when satellites may be more easily available to all.

Perhaps the single controversy which illuminates the struggle over the spectrum more clearly than any other is that over the HF (high frequency—or short wave) band. This band has certain special qualities which make it attractive for very long-distance broadcasting and for a variety of point-to-point services: during the daylight hours the wave propagated on this band travels towards the horizon and is absorbed by the ionosphere; i.e., it disappears into space. At night, however, the ionosphere reflects the wave back to earth which in turn sends it back again, and so on, across thousands of miles. The ITU normally allocates the same wave band simultaneously for different purposes in the three great regions into which it divided the world some decades ago (Europe with Africa, the Americas, and Asia), but in the case of HF, with its long-distance propagation habits, the ITU makes a global set of allocations with special provisions for an extraordinary range of complications stemming from differences of geography and climate, sun-spot activity and other quirks of nature.

The HF frequencies are most noticeably used for international broadcasting but are so valuable that many different services have been allocated a share of them: ship-to-shore and ship-to-ship radio, domestic broadcasting, aeronautical and land mobile services, as well as space research, amateur radio and even the new amateur satellite service. Of the whole of the HF band, broadcasting uses about a tenth, mobile radio about 35 per cent. They are among the oldest frequencies in use and have collected, in various parts of the world, a series of usage anomalies hallowed by time. There are countries which have registered certain frequencies for services which no longer exist, special radio stations operating in the midst of mobile services, or contiguous to them. HF frequencies are greatly favoured by the big international broadcasters such as Voice of America, the BBC, Radio Peking and Voice of the Arabs. An appalling confusion develops at certain times of the day in certain sectors of the globe. Many of the earlier uses of these bands for fixed rather than broadcasting purposes among the developed nations have been abandoned; the telephone engineers of Western Europe used to favour them but have now moved to much higher frequencies with their more advanced equipment. America only employs a few of them now for military purposes.

At the 1979 general WARC, France handed in a large range of fixed-band HF frequencies which had been allotted to her but which were no longer in use because of technological advances. America could probably have handed back a much larger list but her political system, unlike that of France, makes it very difficult for government to remove frequencies from private industrial concerns, which may no longer use them but regard them as part of their fixed capital. It is easy to see how the New International Economic Order and the New International Information Order become intermixed in the discussion over spectrum regulation.

The HF band is clearly over-occupied and is used in its fixed and broadcast sections by a number of very noisy neighbours. The argument is moreover complicated by the demands of the new groups of users and potential users in the developed world; there are companies trying to supply the new demand for mobile services, which is probably the fastest-growing new use for this part of the spectrum. Within a decade or so a very large proportion of motor cars will be equipped with telephones; more and more executives demand 'bleepers'; already police, medical services and many others are demanding the right to exchange information while on the move. The developed world wants to use HF for modern luxuries, the Third World for necessities. The developed world already has much of it registered for abandoned services; developing countries are still opening up their services.

The countries which have come to depend on the HF band more than any other are those of the Third World. African domestic radio, for example, is a heavy user of the broadcast section of the HF band. It is an ideal means for reaching large poor and dispersed populations without having to erect and service a large number of expensive transmitters. It is perfect for linking remote regions to distant transmitters for long-distance policing, for organizing social services across great deserts and for general administrative work in difficult conditions when expensive equipment is not available. The developing nations have seen that the industrialized countries are intent upon spreading modish mobile services in the band. The problem has been which services are to 'move over'. At a special meeting held at Yaounde in the summer of 1979, their representatives declared: 'Developed countries possess more viable and more extensive means to satisfy their needs and could consequently give up the use of HF bands in favour of developing countries.'[3] By the autumn of that year their demands were brought to the WARC in Geneva, and they succeeded by December in obliging the world's representatives to accept certain principles fairly new in frequency planning: it was accepted that developing countries should have more equitable access to frequencies and also that countries should be required to relinquish unused frequencies and 'clean up the Master Register'. For the developing countries the issue was one between haves and have-nots; for the developed world it was a question of permitting new technologies to be developed to the greater benefit of mankind in general—after all, the Third World would also benefit from the mass distribution of mobile communication equipment in the 1980s and 1990s. For the developed countries the problems of HF could be settled through extremely expert planning, but the chief experts familiar with the HF problem were all in the delegations of the industrialized countries and the representatives of Third World countries—some of whom had come to Geneva for the *first ever* experience of telecommunications—had decided to treat the problem as one of justice rather than technical planning. The spectrum, unlike other world resources, is infinite in its possibilities, but the more sophisticated the solution to problems of allocation, the more dependent the less sophisticated users become upon the expertise of the highly developed. The 1979 general WARC was one of the most tense and fraught negotiations over frequencies ever held. It marked the arrival of geo-politics in the electro-magnetic spectrum and left many of the most crucial issues deferred for later conferences. The ITU did, however, remain intact and the basic international system survived, strengthened, perhaps, by the realization of the ordeal it had gone through.

However, we have looked at only one aspect of the HF dispute. There exists a very neat technical solution to overcrowding, which is to use what is called 'single sideband' instead of 'double sideband' transmission. This would mean that new transmitters and new receivers would have to be adapted to the new system for using the waves, but the usefulness of the HF band would be instantly doubled. The USA favours this approach and proposes that the world starts discussing the discontinuation of double sideband transmission after 1995—to the consternation of the Third World. The argument is further complicated in tropical regions where the HF band is allocated in a different manner because of special problems which result from high rainfall and humidity.

The HF band, which is only one small section of the spectrum currently in dispute, is subject to a complexity of arguments comparable to the Schleswig-Holstein questions in the nineteenth century, which, according to Palmerston, had been understood only by three people, one being dead, one driven mad by it while he, the third, had forgotten. Yet buried in the arguments are all the current international tensions over the inequitable distribution of information. The conclusion of the 1979 WARC is by no means the end of the quarrel, which may last until the ITU itself is transformed or politicized in the same way as UNESCO. Its highly technical nature means that it is harder to polarize its discussions, but the intensity of the disagreements could end in precisely similar results. Traditionally, the ITU is an entirely technical and non-political assembly, but today only the complexity of its arguments can safeguard it against steady politicization. 'We hope this strength of ITU will not be compromised by a debate over highly abstract issues of political ideology which are not amenable to resolution at this kind of conference,'[4] said Glen Robinson, WARC Ambassador of the United States in the run-up period to the 1979 WARC. The ITU has been a place where problems are resolved and set aside for long periods of time; political problems are of a different order and are seldom 'settled' after a few weeks' discussion.

The electro-magnetic spectrum happens to be one aspect of international organization which both affects the flow of information and is politically within reach of Third World countries. There are other areas of current decision-making in the information field which are far less accessible. One of them is the area broadly known as 'informatics', the organization of the equipment for the new information services: i.e., the marketing, investment, research and manufacturing activity which result in a society being provided with the means to collect and distribute information. The ability to marshal information in a society is *almost* entirely dependent upon having the appropriate informatics, whether these happen to be computer-operated switching systems in a telephone service or advanced automatic sorting devices in the mailing room of a newspaper. Modern technology has created a myriad of new opportunities and a vast array of new necessities. The problem for any receiving society or receiving company is to ensure that the equipment is selected according to real need rather than to satisfy a salesman, or a foreign diplomat or an irrelevant sense of prestige. It is one thing to consider a telephone system as a necessity, another to demand computer voice recognition on domestic telephone receivers. In some circumstances both are luxuries and in modern circumstances it may be as cheap to acquire the latter as the former if one is starting a system from scratch. A nation needs an educational publishing base of its own, but does it require computer-assisted instruction facilities? It needs a wide selection of specialist and general magazines, but should these be launched with or without on-line text editing and computer composition?

The ability of a nation to plan its information flow has today become almost inextricable from the problem of informatics, in that in many cases the available technology is in conflict, by its nature, with certain national policies. It isn't possible any longer to organize the censorship of incoming journalistic material in a society which, for industrial reasons, has installed advanced equipment for computer data to pass freely across its borders. Where transmission facilities exist, journalistic data will pass from agency computer to newspaper computer and nobody can stop it. It is no longer possible to conceive of technical distinctions between data required for government, industry, banking and newspapers and magazines and if a nation's sense of its own independence and sovereignty is predicated upon control of information, it will experience increasing difficulties. The newspapers of the Irish Republic, for instance, have traditionally prevented the publication of material relating to birth control, and foreign newspapers arriving at Irish ports have even at times had pages removed or have been banned from entering the country if they dealt with the forbidden topics. In a fully computerized newspaper system such controls would be impossible; they belong to the era of Gutenberg which is drawing to a close.

Advanced telecommunications technologies are inexorably linked to data-processing and the social and legal implications are considerable. Even in the United States, where data processing and message sending are statutorily separated and are not supposed to be conducted by the same companies, there is considerable difficulty being experienced in the introduction of certain of the new services which happen to do both at the same time. Viewdata or videotex, for example, is a device run by telephone administrations in Western Europe which may be used for sending personal messages from person to person as well as sending out information from storage computers on request by individuals. It combines the sending of messages (which, in the US, is supposed to be conducted only by 'common carriers', or companies specially permitted this privilege, sometimes as a monopoly) with the editing and publication of messages (which, under the First Amendment, are supposed to be free of governmental supervision and must be subject to open competition).

Even in the most industrialized of countries, therefore, the new informatics raises problems of political conception, issues which may question quite fundamental precepts of the nation's constitution. For developing countries, anxious to preserve the credibility of their insecure regimes and the security of their bureaucracies, the untrammelled flow of data could prove a serious hazard. That does not apply only to countries whose governments regard it as a sovereign duty to impose totalitarian controls on their press; it can pose problems for any society attempting to construct its own indigenous education, banking, credit, newspaper or public library systems. The unhindered flow of data can be an asset or a curse, depending on a society's view of its immediate goals, depending on the ways in which it wishes to develop its independent institutions. A country, for instance, which has chosen to adapt to international subscriber dialling cannot—without prohibitive expense—discriminate against any individual subscriber or organization or prevent the flow of foreign information to any number.

It is very difficult to import informatics without becoming a dumping ground or transit lounge for other societies' information. Modern systems for ferrying data carry the medical, criminal, employment and credit records of individuals; they also carry the data necessary for modern industries, including credit data of private and public companies; they carry the information required by government to plan development. The strands are inextricable, and the companies which control the manufacture of the equipment (which are very few in number) hold the key. There is no longer such a thing as national autonomy without control over data flow and informatics. However much a nation—or all nations—desire to reverse the inequalities in the flow of international news, their intentions are doomed without autonomy in the field of informatics.

One very striking area of development is remote sensing by photo-satellites; NASA's Landsat set of satellites, for example, is able to collect information about the resources of developing countries without communicating it to them. American corporations are able to use the knowledge for their own benefit, and acquire the data freely under the Freedom of Information Act. The country about which the information is circulating may have been attempting, for reasons of its own, to retain strict secrecy about a mineral deposit or the state of its harvest. It might, on the other hand, have no knowledge of the mineral deposit concerned but in present circumstances be unable to prevent the information spreading, long before the authorities are able to inspect the terrain concerned and decide upon a national policy. US mining companies (or any other mining companies who happen to acquire the information) may hurry to take options on tracts of land before the local government has awakened to their mineral riches. According to UN resolution 626 (VII), no nation may 'impede the exercise of sovereignty of any state over its natural resources'; but remote sensing satellites, it may be argued, lead to precisely this result. There is no way to stop them, although it might be possible to argue that all information collected should be transmitted immediately to the country concerned before being published. But without the facilities for receiving the data, processing it and analysing it expertly, what use would such a provision be?

There is no easy common line of approach for developing countries towards informatics. The airlines' booking systems for internal domestic flights of many European countries (including Hungary, Poland and Czechoslovakia) depend upon a computer sited in Texas. The information required by the fire service in Malmö, Sweden, is kept in a special database in Florida. The personnel records of most transnational companies are held in the country where the company has its headquarters. Where there is a degree of data interdependence—say between Canada and the US—the process is less damaging, although Canada is today rapidly moving towards great insistence on domestic data storage. Where nations are not interdependent in anything but name, there could be a great deal of autonomy lost in the process of moving into the new informatics. Yet neither a firm policy of total insistence upon indigenous control of data nor a policy of free flow of data will help in all instances. Airlines must have computerized booking and the computer concerned may just happen to be in Atlanta.

What is opening up for the world is a whole new field of domestic policy-making. Many countries, both North and South, have already embarked upon it. Clearly, they must and will regulate certain imports of equipment which will tend to destabilize the process of national development; they will also inevitably impose controls on certain exports. Secondly, they will have to participate much more forcefully than before in the international community to ensure that the field of international law evolves in a manner which suits them: they cannot simply lie down and allow the 'market' system of the developed world to crush them. Thirdly, they will band together for increased power, either regionally, or geo-politically or just ideologically; while there is a need for technology transfer from the developed countries, there is a great deal of scope for mutual technology transfer among the developing. But more than all of these there is a need for each nation to design its own policy in the light of its own cultural predilections: the balance between centralization and federal decisions, between regional and local, between indigenous and imported, between free flow and control is one which only each individual nation can hold for itself. India, for example, informed IBM that it wanted 51 per cent of its interests there and IBM replied that it must have all or nothing and left the country in 1978; India is now attempting to make its own computers in government-owned companies. It might or might not work, but it would be wrong to view its decision not to allow its domestic computer market to disappear into the maw of IBM (as has that of most of the world) as a mere anti-American issue.

Oddly enough, the field of informatics, which represents the developed world at its most inexorably powerful, is also one in which the same countries are very vulnerable. For if the transformation of Western industrial economies or information economies is to succeed, they must eventually enjoy the benefits of a free flow of data. If an era of high data tariffs were to dawn or forms of severe data restriction be imposed at international borders, the whole development of informatics would be hampered. At certain levels of the technology, the world will find itself in a state of real interdependence, which the developing nations can exploit to their advantage. For the latter it is really a last chance to reattain an evaporating sovereignty, which in turn is the key to social and economic development; for those developed nations, in which the manufacture of information goods is already the third or fourth largest industry, it is a new chance to reinject dynamism into the capitalist order.

The issue of trans-border data flow is one which concerns developed and developing nations alike. One Canadian newspaper report on the subject recently declared, 'The US may soon own all our secrets—unless we start insisting that computerized information stay this side of the border.'[5] Several provinces in Canada have already passed laws preventing the movement of data beyond provincial jurisdiction, and in April 1979 a Consultative Committee on the Implications of Telecommunications for Canadian Sovereignty proposed a new blanket programme of regulation and national education on the problem. A federal prohibition on the exportation of data would have to be co-ordinated with the planned training of systems analysts, programmers and others needed for creating Canadian substitute systems.

One incident which has added urgency to the problem has been a case which came before the House of Lords in London in 1977 after a US official prosecutor wanted to take evidence in Britain from an official of a Crown Corporation which was before an American court on charges relating to financial management. The Lords confirmed the decision of lower courts that questioning British subjects on British territory by agents of a foreign government would constitute an infringement of sovereignty. It was wondered at the time whether this piece of sovereignty could have been protected if the information concerned had been held in a computer stored under American control. Any information stored within America, even if it belongs to some other nation or to a foreign company, or affects the territorial rights of another nation, will none the less fall under American jurisdiction and could be 'extradited' or subpoenaed by an American court. The same argument might apply to computer data which was in the process of being bounced off an American satellite, even if the data were starting and finishing their journey on non-American territory. The whole history of the nation as a political unit of mankind has been predicated upon territoriality; the technology of printing came into being in the same era as the nation-state and both seem to be reaching the end of their usefulness in the era of the computer; it is physically impossible to impose upon data the same kinds of controls that are imposed upon goods and paper-borne information, though the world will inevitably continue to try to do so for some years.

Brazil, the Philippines, Venezuela and Mexico have all passed measures in recent years designed to impose some kind of notional or theoretical control over foreign data links, at least in regard to certain crucial industries (e.g. Venezuelan oil). However, the passing of laws may not in itself help matters, since a great deal of data cannot really be said to be 'stored' in any one place. It flits about the globe from computer to computer, 'packet-switched' from destination to destination, depending on available routes and available capacity. It is not the case that all data has a final resting place like files on a shelf. It defies territoriality, however hard national governments may seek to pin it down.

The Intergovernmental Bureau of Informatics has been working towards some kind of international agreement on trans-border data flow and is to hold a world conference in 1980 in Rome to discuss the problem. It conducted a survey of interested countries and identified thirty-five which had already announced an intention to regulate such flows by means of special laws going beyond the normal controls of their national telecommunications administrations.[6] It remains to be seen how these nations propose to go about the task and how a world organization may succeed in tackling it. Data has become as slippery as mercury and as unregulatable as the sea. A recent Swedish national report on the subject was entitled 'The Vulnerable Society', which conveys a sense of the helpless riskiness which surrounds the topic.[7]

There is a further fear which lies behind the anxieties of the developed countries towards trans-border data flow. In these countries, which are dedicated to 'free flow' as a general principle, there has been and will continue to be a great deal of domestic legislation designed to protect privacy, protect citizens against the free dissemination of credit-checking data, prevent the open circulation of police files on individuals and generally safeguard society against various forms of computer-based surveillance by public authorities and private companies. Certain organizations have been planning to set up 'data–havens' in developing countries or other countries prepared to take a 'rogue' line on data; information, the distribution of which would be illegal in one or more countries, could be held on-line in countries which have a legal 'vacuum'. Developing countries may be tempted to afford this privilege to illegal operators in exchange for rental. World agreement on international control of data is therefore all the more urgent.

The loss of data by a nation also means loss to balance of payments and employment. Canadian ministers have claimed that the country has been losing information processing business to the tune of $150–300 million per year, in addition to 30–40,000 jobs, simply as a result of the outflow of Canadian data into the United States. Salary clerks, banking and administrative facilities, book-keeping and filing personnel have been eliminated not by the introduction of new technology in itself so much as by reason of the fact that computers have been located in the United States and it has become convenient to perform physical and data processing tasks at the same locations. It is not difficult to imagine the impact upon developing countries, where office work conceals a great deal of unemployment, of the transfer of administrative data to storage in a developed society. There are already 300 million people—in a formal sense—unemployed in Third World countries.

In this area, the French government has come up with valuable proposals. They have noted that international information exchange evades customs posts and customs duties which physical goods would have to pay and that information is not identified in trade statistics. It would be possible, therefore, to create a new kind of tax levied on the value of information transactions between organizations working in different countries. Since data replaces physical workers whose earnings would have been subject to income tax, it would seem appropriate to find some means for bringing information flows inside the general orbit of taxation. The new information economy is still coming into place and it might be a little too soon yet to discern exactly how this could be achieved.

What many observers and researchers have noticed is the way in which a variety of quite different problems—relating to particular branches of informatics, to copyright and other legal matters, to freedom of information questions, to taxation and to technology transfer questions—are all coming together into a single amalgamated complex of policy questions, which one might simply label the Information Problem. One has only to examine the new laws which have been enacted in half a dozen countries and the guidelines being formulated in others for new legislation to see how interconnected these matters are becoming, as the progress of informatics reorganizes the agenda of human society. Already America exports over $5 billion worth of information equipment and services a year—quite apart from her production for domestic use. Japan is not far behind. It is not surprising that so colossal an intrusion into trade figures is bringing in its train a welter of political and international conundrums.

III

At the centre of the information problem lies the figure of IBM. It is responsible for 70 per cent of all computer installations in the entire globe. In 1978, its revenue from the rental of computers was $10 billion and profits from this sector accounted for half of its entire profits. Within the United States, IBM is not permitted to sell computer services such as data processing. However, it has a $1 billion a year overseas trade in selling computer services. It employs 130,000 workers in plants outside the United States. In nearly all of the developed countries IBM has at least 50 per cent of the total computer market. Even in Japan, which is well on the way to self-sufficiency in computer hardware, IBM still has over a quarter of the market. It is the power of IBM which helps to explain the extra-ordinary predominance of the USA in the information field. [8]

If a count is made of the records held in the computerized data-bases of the world (something which inevitably has to be something of a guess rather than an estimate), it is clear that America holds nearly nine-tenths of them (46 million out of 52 million). Of America's share, one quarter are records of the US government, 35 per cent are those of commercial organizations and 40 per cent of non-commercial bodies. Three-quarters of all records held in computers are directly or indirectly related to science and technology and most of the overlap between US governmental and scientific material is accounted for by military research in the US. [9]

It is not surprising that the countries of the EEC have become acutely aware of the dangers of increasing dependence in an area in which regional, if not national independence is essential. The foundation of EURONET was a reaction to this. It is a consortium of national computer interests in nine countries working towards the creation of a mutually compatible interconnection of European databases. EURONET is designed for reasons which are as much political as economic as a method for ensuring that in the long run the economic control of Europe remains in European hands. The problem of transborder data flows has long exercised the mind of OECD, which called a conference as early as 1977 to discuss ways of international regulation. A group of fifty Americans attended the conference and *Computerworld*[10] reported that this contingent had 'won' because the conference ended without any particular form of international restriction of data flow being recommended. As an American businessman said to a Congressional Committee: 'We alone are not fully aware that we are at economic war with the rest of the world. We will do our nation a disservice if we don't elevate this discussion.'[11]

Some of the new projects in satellite-borne communications will have the effect of greatly reducing the costs of administering trans-national organizations and organizations whose plants and offices are spread across a wide area. By transmitting their internal written communications (orders, memos, internal invoices, etc.) via satellites, very great savings in costs can be achieved and dependence upon the physical postal services can be eliminated. Electronic mail is one of the most significant innovations for future systems, but for the foreseeable future it will be suitable only for the internal traffic of large organizations; personal mail and a great deal of the material which is distributed to private houses through the physical post will for a long time continue in its present mode, although the advent of domestic computing could lead to a great deal of computer-generated mail, bills in particular (which accounts for 30–40 per cent of first class mail in the more advanced countries), by-passing the physical stage of transport and entering the home via a screen.

It is on the field of intra-corporate communications that the pioneers of electronic mail are setting their sights. The Hewlett-Packard Corporation, for example, has already created its own internal electronic mail system which has, according to the company's own calculations, enabled it to take on orders at a far higher rate than would have been possible if it had remained totally dependent on US and other postal services. Its plants are distributed in several continents; it has 4,000 different products and hundreds of thousands of parts on its order books at any given moment. It has reduced its internal invoicing and ordering to a series of standardized sheets and an enormous volume (hundreds of thousands per day) of messages are being transferred from postal services to electronic mode. Already, about 12 million words a day pass through the headquarters of this intra-corporate system at Palo Alto, California, from ninety-four separate centres. In due course it will not be necessary for everything to pass through a single central point, and Hewlett-Packard will move into the phase of being a 'dispersed corporation' an organization for whom electronic communications afford the opportunity of total decentralization. A new enterprise form is, in a sense, coming into existence, which differs in significant respects from the transnational company, its immediate forebear.

The most important single aid to this evolution now being planned is SBS—Satellite Business Systems—a company formed by IBM, Comsat (the US communications satellite company) and Aetna Life Insurance Company. Its plans have been shrouded in discreet corporate public relations for several years, perhaps awaiting the outcome of the 1979 WARC, since its life depends upon the allocation of a suitable set of frequencies in the 12–14 gigahertz band which has been set aside for ground to satellite data links, both for direct broadcasting and fixed satellites. SBS has been 'grand-fathering' a frequency in this band (squatting on it prior to allocation, in the hope that its right to continue using the frequency will be eventually conceded) since 1978. SBS is really the latest phase in the long struggle between the giant AT&T, which is the principal American common carrier for public telecommunication services, and IBM. The new system will offer large corporations the chance to send all of their messages—letters, invoices, filing systems, computer data and telex and telephone services—by way of the satellite to small ground stations situated on the premises of the companies concerned. From these local points telephone calls can be sent through AT&T's normal system. SBS is capable of transmitting an enormous volume of traffic, all of which, in effect, would be business taken away from the US postal system and AT&T. No longer would a company have to rely on outside governmental bodies for its internal communications; its external communications would be vastly cheapened too and in due course SBS would be able to offer cheap communication between companies and across national frontiers, when regulations permit.

SBS is not only, however, a blow for communications cheapness, instantaneity and corporate autonomy. It is also a blow against all the new competitors of IBM which have sprung up in Europe, Japan and the developing countries. All companies using the new internal communications system based on SBS would have to use IBM's computer installations. The new mini-computer movement might even be crippled, since it will become cheaper to use the capacity of a distant mainframe computer of the kind IBM specializes in, once the heavy costs of normal telecommunications links (as previously provided through AT&T) are eliminated.

So far, SBS's services are conceived as intra-corporate. But it is important to note the role of Comsat in the trio of entrepreneurs behind SBS. At the present time a great deal of thought is being given in the United States to the rewriting of the 1934 Communications Act, which is the basic law on which the regulation of telecommunications of all kinds (including radio and television) in the United States is based. The proposals of Congressman Van Deerlin have been widely encouraged but not yet accepted by Congress, despite two years of attempts on the part of his committee to 'deregulate' a great number of telecommunication services. When the rewriting of this act is ultimately approved (although no date can be put on it), the Intelsat Treaty could be altered to permit Comsat —a hitherto domestic agency—to sell satellite services overseas as well as internally. At this point SBS, firmly seated on the spectrum and capable of generating and processing a much greater volume of traffic than that afforded by US intra-corporate business, will be able to move into the field of international mail and telephone connection, replacing the cumbersome unreliable services of many countries with instant and reliable communication, both on paper and in sound. The whole of filing systems of corporations around the world could be stored in IBM computers situated anywhere in the world. Where data links are presently costly and clogged with traffic between continents and across oceans they will become ridiculously cheap, by traditional standards, and plentiful.

The problems of sovereignty and indigenous control will, however, be multiplied to an extent that is presently difficult even to comprehend. It will be possible, no doubt, for governments, universities, authorities of all kinds to make use of the system. It will present a challenge to the autonomy of every institution in modern society, from law courts, police, education, business management, banking, insurance, and every function in society which does not entail the physical manufacture of goods. It is scarcely conceivable that the concept of national sovereignty as currently understood could survive for many decades. One of the earliest national institutions over which the nation-state insisted on maintaining monopoly was the postal system. In modern circumstances, each postal and telecommunications administration retains the right to intercept communication between the different parts of a great transnational corporation in order to enforce laws on taxation, privacy, etc. One great fear is that developing nations could be tempted to do deals with SBS in their anxiety to obtain its cheap and reliable services, perhaps in exchange for the offer of help for governmental communications, and will only later discover the extent to which they have become dependent upon Comsat and IBM. Countries like Indonesia, with its Hughes Aircraft-built 'Palapa' satellite, have already begun to realize how many of their national communication services (telephones, data, newspaper content, education) have come to rely on the satellite, which ultimately still remains in the control of NASA, which launched it, as well as the company which manufactured it. No nation is secure against coercion which is not secure against eavesdropping and modern communications systems are in this sense always vulnerable to the nations and organizations which have created them. Even with the most sophisticated encryption devices, it is not impossible for ingenious outsiders to break the code.

At a conference organized at the instigation of President Giscard d'Estaing in Paris in September 1979, Henry Geller, Assistant Secretary for Communication and Information in the Carter

Administration, spoke to an audience of European information experts about the differences between the American and European approaches to transborder data flow. 'We regard the free flow of information as a principle of first importance. We recognize that it isn't absolute—indeed, any scheme of privacy protection derogates from it—but it is the starting point and the continuing goal against which other information objectives are to be achieved.' Geller had already explained the FCC's thinking which had led it to permit the SBS operation in 1977 and to reject its opponents' claim that SBS would tend to diminish competition (based on the idea that SBS, in joining together a data processing company (IBM) and a common carrier (Comsat), by its very nature undermined the competitive system). The pro-competitive, pro-free flow implication of SBS is that it brings about competition with AT&T and that is consistent with the tenor of modern American thinking. 'We want to avoid bureaucratic and governmental control mechanisms, the regulation of data processing or computer industries, and unnecessary or excessive expense and delay.' The thrust of Geller's speech, and that of members of the Van Deerlin Congressional Committee also, was that the opening up of competition between the giant American concerns operating in information is the only way to render them publicly accountable and at the same time to enable society to derive benefit from the new technology quickly. 'Instead of there being a largely monopolistic market limited to one or two major firms, we see a highly dynamic competitive market with new firms entering and existing firms free to exit.'

It is, furthermore, becoming increasingly difficult for the existing official regulatory body, the FCC, to distinguish between those forms of communication which are subject to regulation and data processing which is not subject to it. Technology is increasingly bringing together the function of running networks with the function of performing services by way of those networks and the only possible response of American society is to open up both to competition rather than strangle the whole development by bringing both within range of regulation. Moreover, the whole international development of the Western economy depends upon this expansion of the information sector:

The fact is that our economies in the West are so closely integrated by the telecommunications and computer networks now in existence that to function in the modern world without constant data exchanges would be quite impossible. In the United States we are concerned about growing signs of protectionism and administrative/governmental policy inhibiting telecommunications and data processing industries in the development of facilities and services.[12]

Clearly, other nations will not see the future in quite the same way, although a 'de-regulatory' mood is sweeping over much of Western Europe, including Britain under the Thatcher administration. In forcing its transnational giants into an intensified competition, America is in effect inducing them to challenge further the indigenous control of data in all of the countries across which the American giants will conduct their economic warfare. For the market over which the competition will take place is not merely that of the United States, but the whole of the rest of the world. The globe is thus to become a battlefield for the corporate competition of America's information giants. That may not be wholly a bad thing; it may bring more efficient services and spur more countries to develop and rationalize their own industry to compete. But the lower down the scale of development the more likely is a society to be the victim of this competition rather than a participant. Certain societies may lose such free control as they presently exercise over their own economic destiny. All societies will have to think very hard about how to regulate against the worst effects of American de-regulation. What seems to be a liberal cause in America can bring out illiberal forces in other societies, in favour of more and more governmental control, and the latter may be absolutely correct in their own terms. All autonomy is at stake in the era of competition between the information transnationals.

It is right to draw attention to the corporate and financial changes in America of which the information revolution consists. Since the 1950s the American telephone companies have provided one quarter of all new public equity in the US during a period of immense economic growth—in 1979 alone it amounted to $3 billion in public stock.[13] The changes in regulatory methods to which Henry Geller referred will mean that the neat vertically integrated AT&T concern will break up as the new technologies proceed; i.e., the capital structure of this enormous industry will undergo total transformation. Until now, AT&T has held up to 50 per cent of the total debt of the entire telecommunications industry, safe as it has been against all forms of competition; it has, as a general policy, subsidized expensive local telephone calls, with their low profit margins, with profits from lucrative long-distance services where the rates have been kept artificially high. The 'long-lines' are now subject to fierce competition from newcomers. Until the computer companies entered the business of building exchanges, AT&T was also the unassailed manufacturing giant in this field (through its control of Western Electric); here, too, competition from new computer firms is skimming off the more profitable sections of the business, leaving AT&T with the less profitable mainframe business. AT&T's response has been to start a policy of reducing its vast debt burden by massively reinvesting its own dividends. Meanwhile, it is becoming clear that de-regulation will oblige AT&T to lose much of the terminal equipment business (i.e., telephones and ancillary equipment) to the new companies in the field, and this in turn means a switch from leasing to purchase, which will reduce AT&T's need to finance the production business. The write-off period for billions of dollars worth of equipment is now being dramatically reduced since the new computerized equipment (as produced, for example, by IBM) is written off in much less than the twenty years customary in the telecommunications business; the banks are now coming in to provide a much larger proportion of all future finance across the industry and the new companies will be searching for fresh cash-flows with which to service bank debts for decades to come.

The growth of the telecommunications industry has been and will continue to be three times as great as that of the economy as a whole, but where the growth has occurred under the protection of governmental regulation, it will now be taking place across a haphazard unplanned multitudinous corporate scene. The first response of American business to de-regulation will be a wave of corporate acquisitions as new blocks of capital search for quick ways to enter this extraordinarily vital area of business activity. Despite the dominance of AT&T's Bell subsidiary in the provision of telephone service, America has contained well over a thousand small telephone companies which are rapidly being consolidated and merged into perhaps 300–400 concerns or even less.

IV

Some writers on these issues, such as Herbert Schiller, have been arguing that computer communications are of general usefulness but are neither necessary nor urgent for all societies in the present state of computer development. '. . . It is no less reasonable to believe that a very significant part of what is now regarded as vital record-keeping, requiring vast amounts of information processing, could be dispensed with entirely in a community with different social objectives and different underlying social structures and practice .'[14] This could well be true and it would follow that computer communications is also widening the disparity between nations and *within* developing nations (where local élites become culturally linked with their counterparts in the US and Japan and Europe). It might also be true, as Schiller implies, that computer generations succeed each other so fast and with such dramatic increases in capacity and versatility that developing nations would be well advised to wait.

It can be equally well argued, however, that the gaps which computer technology, at its present stage of development, is creating between rich and poor societies are so great that a failure to catch up with them or to lay the foundations for Third World computing capacity could result in irretrievable backwardness in the early part of the next century. Third World countries have to map out their own path to development if they are to develop at all. The issue remains one of independence, as the Europeans have perceived. Simon Nora and Alain Minc of the French Finance Ministry, who wrote the important national report for France on the problem, 'L'Informatisation de la Société',[15] advised of the need to challenge IBM and contain it. With independence once lost, the economies of whole continents, not to speak of individual nations, could be cajoled into unwanted economic alliances offering little benefit to their population. It is by no means clear that it is possible to leap on the escalator at a later stage, even though it is difficult to see at a given moment in development exactly which parts of the information society should be adapted by a given Third World society. Brazil and India, however, have taken certain very clear steps: they have decided to embark upon computer industries of their own and have decided that all imports of computers must be scrutinized by government and given prior approval. Even Brazilian subsidiaries of American transnationals have been instructed to buy locally constructed computers instead of importing from IBM, even though this would prevent them linking with the parent company in the United States.

An apposite example of the kind of threat to national economic policy-making posed to trans-border flows of data is in the computerized banking systems called SWIFT (Society for World Financial Information Transactions); this system operates daily bank clearing work in a single worldwide market and has begun to transform world money flow. It means that cash can be moved around the world with extreme speed and without any hindrance being placed through physical or legal obstacles. It holds 300,000 transactions at a time, some of considerable size, beyond all national supervision. The entire 'bank' is run on a computer which generates a kind of stateless currency, rocketing about the globe, potentially creating international currency instability as it moves. If this system acquired large sums it could bring catastrophe to struggling currencies in the course of an afternoon. In the hands of a hostile power (a government or a transnational company intent on taking revenge upon a small country attempting, say, to substitute local manufactures for cheaper imports) SWIFT could be a devastating tool. As well as causing currency and stock fluctuations, such devices can create a kind of electronic 'free port' where funds can be placed in unregulated markets. Clearly the policy of most governments in the world, including many industrialized societies, has simply not yet taken measure of the problems incurred by trans-border flows of data.

What is at stake today is nationhood. The repertoire of techniques now available to companies which are essentially uncontrolled by any national entity and are therefore effectively unassailable by any single set of laws is such as to negate the possibility of secure nationhood for any who permit the unquestioned flow of data across their borders. The industrialized countries have some power of riposte because they house at least meaningful quantities of data and may generate larger amounts. They can bargain with IBM almost as equals. This is not the case with the larger part of the developing world for whom national independence could become little more than an empty phrase substantiated by military power.

The view commonly held of Third World countries by kindly Westerners is still that they are just like industrialized countries only lagging behind, like teenagers who need a little extra coaching after school. What they need is simply to be 'modernized'. It is an historically exploded view but it is probably the commonest. It tends to go with the notion that the export of 'expertise' from Western to developing countries will serve to provide the missing catalytic ingredient which will somehow pitchfork the laggard nation into an era of permanent growth which will result inevitably in democracy, mass literacy and prosperity.

If anything, the experience of the last twenty years has taught that the transference of technology raises a multitude of problems for the most part unforeseen by the development experts of the post-colonial period. Many of the technologies which have been transferred from the West in the 1960s and 1970s have turned out to be excessively capital intensive and have tended to introduce to the countries concerned an organizational pattern of distorted centralization and tending towards the concentration of wealth. Western technology has promised general improvement only on the 'trickle down' principle; it has been built around a new élite of urban businessmen and bureaucrats. What many countries have come round to feeling is that they need only technologies which combine the maximum amount of employment with the minimum amount of investment—'appropriate technology' in the current jargon.

Among the apostles of the new idea has of course been E. F. Schumacher, who argued cogently in North and South for 'appropriate technology', having acquired many of his ideas during his years of experience working in Asian aid programmes. The basic idea which he and his followers have adopted is that basic human needs must be satisfied at the level of the village, rather than the capital city. But what is 'appropriate' in the field of information? Is it the creation of paper mills and local printing presses in order to found a small-scale newspaper industry, or is it the use of half-inch video tape which reduces the level of skilled professionalism required but places maintenance and replacement beyond the scope of the village society? The dilemma is whether to transfer technology at a labour-intensive level, reached by America and Europe in the nineteenth century, or to offer an advanced but small-scale technology which is extremely cheap but creating a certain dependence. The Indian SITE satellite television project used half-inch video, transmitted programmes across an enormous area and involved a number of villagers in the task of producing the programmes. In a sense, it combined high and low technology in a single programme.

In the communications field, development experts of the 'appropriate' school say there must be community media: small cassette recorders, rural newspapers, low-power radio stations, the use of super-8 film equipment. They argue that this is the only way to avoid the crippling effects of professionalism which are automatically imported alongside the large-scale media used in the West. A country which tries to start, for example, a massive television centre, with signals reaching out around the country and links from city to city, will find itself importing alongside the equipment a sense of the need for an exaggerated professionalism, inappropriate to the conditions of a developing society, though deemed essential in other societies where the same equipment is used. Big media force the 'trickle down' principle upon the receiving society and create social and economic distortions and a reliance upon a small, alienated urban elite. The trouble is that the high technology of today tends to make societies dependent upon Western suppliers and often upon satellites, as the Indian experiment showed. There is a terrible dilemma here, one which will inevitably increase in intensity as the next stage in the evolution in electronic communications takes place.

The satellite enables developing societies to link themselves together. It enables lateral transfer as well as vertical transfer of technology and information to take place—something which, as we saw earlier, the colonial heritage has rendered very difficult through traditional media. Where there is a shortage of simple telephone links between Asia, Africa and South America, satellite technology can provide universal linkages at a tiny fraction of the cost in money and labour. But it means that more and more functions within the linked societies become dependent upon a foreign-built satellite. The same satellite can create the framework for a mass of community media across large tracts of territory where television signals of the ordinary kind would take decades to reach. But does a country want to become so dependent upon a stranger satellite? The Indian SITE experiment came, stayed for a year, and was then switched off, amid Indian hopes for a new satellite for a bigger experiment some years later. The Indians are now preparing their own space programme and insisted, even at the time of the SITE experiment, on constructing all the terrestrial hardware and software within India itself. But it is not possible for every developing society to create such an infrastructure and most will inevitably simply open themselves up as vast markets for Japanese and American and other exports of equipment as soon as the satellite starts beaming its signals across their lands.

As long ago as the Bandung Conference of 1955 the call went up for the mutual reconnecting of developing societies. The era of colonialism had led in fact to a cessation of trading links between countries of the South which had taken place for centuries. The great civilizations of East Africa and Asia were all engaged in a large amount of mutual shipping and trading—the whole of it destroyed in the course of a few years by invaders from Europe who had no idea what they were disrupting; indeed, they wondered why their plundered victims suddenly became poor and 'backward' after their arrival. The restitution of such links in the late twentieth century would, in a sense, be an act of historic justice; satellite and advanced underseas cable are two means which are presently available. Such steps would further assist the development of such new phenomena as Brazilian firms tendering for African building contracts; they have succeeded because similarities in climate and stages of development give the Brazilians an edge in appropriate experience over contractors from the industrialized North.

Certainly, the ideal of the 1980s in Third World development lies in technical co-operation among developing countries (TCDC). The whole mood of the international debate about technology transfer is changing in favour of the mutual transfer between countries at similar stages of development; the industrialized world is then expected to provide its technology with greater consideration for the actual human context in which it is to function. There are few fields in which the principle of TCDC should be applied more punctiliously than that of communications. Indeed, ways of rendering advanced communications systems more appropriate to the developing world were among the most urgent items on the agenda of the MacBride Commission when it set to work in 1978. Mustapha Masmoudi, in the early stages of the commission's work, insisted that it should consider the terms of a possible international code of conduct governing the transfer of technology which would correspond more closely to the needs of developing societies; he maintained also that the whole mode by which access is opened up to modern technologies should be made more appropriate to the varying needs of the widely varied receivers. The intention was not to diminish by any means the level of technical aid but rather to create a vastly different approach to means and ends.[16]

Towards the end of 1978, the conference held in Spain under the auspices of the IBI (Intergovernmental Bureau of Informatics) gave a further impetus to the cause of technological transfer between developed and developing countries.[17] It was evident that enormous pressure was bound to be exerted on the informatics-producing countries to adapt their wares, to make them available for appropriate tasks and to undertake all the relevant training and research activity, which would later result in a mutually satisfactory form of transfer. What has not been made so clear is the way in which the natural bias of informatics acts towards the distortion of cultures, the loss of ethnic identity. It is questionable whether computerization in general is an aid or a hindrance to pluralism. In an unequal world the information revolution renders a wide array of cultures extremely vulnerable.

The IBI has been active, for example, in helping the Arab countries to acquire computer terminals which function in the Arabic alphabet, an adjustment which will certainly in time prove practicable. One has to ask, none the less, whether this will make the Middle East cultures and societies more or less available for Western economies to dominate. Will this apparent move towards autonomy in informatics act as a syphon through which the great corporations of the West will extract the data of developing societies even before complete sovereignty is achieved? Will it provide a real opportunity for a two-way flow of data and understanding? Data processing, by its nature, reduces the world to the crude terms of information; it is an intellectually biased tool. Yet fully developed countries can acquire a kind of privacy, retain a local identity, adopt an approach of their own to the storage of data. An American and a French database are recognizably American and French; the intellectual differences of style and history do find their counterparts in the new knowledge structures. Dependence of any kind, however, tends to be magnified in the changeover to informatics, which have emerged from the needs of sophisticated industrialized societies.

The Third World has no choice, of course, but to enter this age of history; perhaps the only uncertainty is over the extent to which it will be crippled by the process of modernization. At the conference organized in Paris in September 1979 by President Giscard d'Estaing to discuss the age of informatics, a delegate from Senegal said that the computer profoundly reflected the societies from which it sprang: Western society always seemed to have destroyed direct personal relationships and as the computer advanced he thought that the West would lose even more of the personal sphere in favour of the structured non-emotional world of impersonal 'interface'. It was a statement which most of the Western delegates would have been embarrassed to make, although it was one which must have passed through the minds of everyone present at least fleetingly during the week of reports and debates. Are computer games—allegedly enjoyed immensely by the children of computer pioneers—a fitting substitute for the games of childhood? Is the proposed universality of the computer a profound impoverishment of the affective life?

Even if there is only a little truth in this fear the emotional damage will be very much greater in societies which have not yet even acquired the social and cultural patterns of the industrialized world. The challenge to national sovereignty posed by direct broadcasting satellites, remote sensing and transborder data flow, is a mere outward expression of a challenge to the human sensibility. Those cultures which are condemned to be the observed rather than the observers may in this, as in other matters, turn out to be not the beneficiaries of modernity, but rather the victims.

5. Double Standards of Freedom?

In November 1976, Tanzania announced the foundation of its new national news agency. Reuters had designed the agency and trained its staff in London. But the policy of TNA, as it was called, was that it was to be responsible for 'counter-measures against imperialist news dissemination' and to 'uphold, support and justify confidence' in the government of Tanzania. TNA was provided from its birth with a monopoly of the distribution of foreign news in Tanzania and also of the collection and dissemination of news at home. The design is not at all dissimilar to the news monopolies constructed by late Tudor monarchs in England. The activities of all foreign correspondents in Tanzania were to be subjected to permits and authorization and it was to be illegal for any citizen to distribute news about Tanzania or cause it to be distributed abroad. This was no notional control system. There were already half a dozen journalists in jail in Tanzania; some of them had been held without trial for years.

Despite the policy and the coercive force which lay behind it, this was to be no totalitarian or propaganda venture on the part of the government in Dar-es-Salaam, but an exercise in 'developmental news', with an emphasis on spreading an understanding of the ideology of Tanzanian socialism. The purpose of its journalism was to go further than mere accuracy, objectivity and balance and to become a means by which the Tanzanian people are led towards the goals of development.

It is difficult for a citizen of the West to discover the words with which to describe this approach towards journalism without being either satirical or craven. It is possible—just possible, but certainly not easy—to see the distinction between a deliberate social role for news reporting and a journalism which is merely supportive of a government or ruling party. The distance between Leninist journalism and developmental journalism is an important one; developmental journalism was, and is, one of the surviving idealistic goals of the 1960s, when it seemed possible to build new institutions entirely from grassroots, and to create in the Third World a kind of village counterpart to the 'alternative press' of Paris, New York, Los Angeles, Berlin, London, Amsterdam. Some of those Asian journalists who were the first to formulate this new doctrine have subsequently repudiated it, after seeing the travesties of objective and professional journalism which have emerged in its name. To be fair, a number of projects started up in Asia and in Africa mainly financed on grants from Western foundations, which have produced durable though impoverished magazines and specialist agencies.

In francophone Africa there exists one such project, Famille et Développement, which circulates information concerning health and family planning, rigorously eschewing all other political messages and managing to keep a circulation of 25,000 spread over a number of countries. It is lively and effective, helping to awaken communities with low literacy to a grasp of basic hygiene and to the business of public discussion. But there is an enormous difference between this very special kind of journal, which avoids all confrontation with power, and, on the one hand, the free press of Europe, America, Japan, and, on the other, the Third World press which is subject to government monitoring. An older generation of Asian journalists, who have pioneered a European-style non-governmental press in India, Thailand, Singapore—in between bouts of governmental oppression—is fading away today, perhaps feeling that they have planted the seeds of an ungrowable plant. In their place there has sprung a new generation of journalists highly trained in a technical sense but subject to a profoundly different view of journalistic possibilities. It was the Prime Minister of Guyana who said in 1975 that journalism in developing countries can only be a means for 'pushing the development of the nation in the context of governmental policy'. To him and to other politicians of his generation, it now seems that regimentation of printed press and broadcasting is a *sine qua non* of political order. Where economic growth has been impossible to achieve at a rate necessary for political contentment, it is easy to see why governments will take no risk with their information policies.

There can be little doubt that in due course the Third World will become embroiled in national struggles for a free press. The journalists of many developing societies are clearly ready for such a fight, though it may still be a long time coming. It took Europe centuries to develop the press doctrine of the 'fourth estate'. There were long struggles and even a number of revolutions fought out principally over the demand for an independent press. But in Vienna in 1848 and in Paris in 1830 and 1870 it was at least feasible for newspapers to be owned by groups of citizens or individuals who were directly caught up in opposing sides of the political life of the society. In

Africa, Asia and South America, a non-governmental press can only at present be a foreign-owned press. With a number of important exceptions, only governments have the resources to set up newspapers and magazines and to organize their distribution, and governments are not likely to create organizations deliberately to confront themselves. Yet within the Third World today there really do exist different views of the possible role of journalism, in addition to the inherited practices and doctrines of a competitive, objective press.

Kenya, Nigeria and India, for example, are countries in which critical journalism has certainly taken root, despite government controls and/or foreign ownership. Both Nigeria and Ghana are returning after military rule to the principle of a free press, with governments agreeing to sell newspaper shares back to private proprietors. In Accra, the Essah Committee, set up to look into the conditions of service of journalists, has argued that the duty of journalists 'can only be discharged if the government recognizes at all times the journalist's right to seek the public interest as he sees it. The government ought not to order journalists to print or suppress news, to refrain from commenting on any issue, or in any way to pervert the truth. Unpleasant facts do not disappear by being swept under the carpet. They merely fester.' Joe Rodrigues, Editor-in-Chief of the Nation group of newspapers with headquarters in Nairobi, noted at a conference of the International Press Institute that the swing away from totalitarian press theory was becoming clear. He quoted himself as having said in February 1979: 'I do not believe that in any independent African country a newspaper editor can say to himself he will operate under the "publish and be damned" doctrine and expect to get away with it.' But by the summer of the same year he had seen that times were changing; totalitarian and dictatorial regimes were passing and:

> It was dawning on those who seek to impose their wills and ways on the media that there need not be perpetual deadlock in their relations, and that cooperation in news flow can function to their mutual benefit. . . . We must not relax our vigilance in the pursuit of ways and means of guaranteeing the free flow of news, but by the same token [we must] refuse to surrender to the argument that nothing can be done to bring the opposing schools of thought together.[1]

It was perhaps typical that a Kenyan should see the way through the ideological impasse as one of compromise and eclecticism. None the less, the period of news suppression in Africa in the 1970s has brought its own disillusionments, even to those who have most fervently believed in the necessity of a 'guided' journalism. One may not predict how far the pendulum will swing and how long the press will retain the protection of a renewed doctrine of freedom, but it will certainly have a great deal to do with the evolution of professional practices. The fusion between freedom and responsibility in the special context of a developing society with economic and political insecurities can only emerge from the activity of free journalists who choose to work responsibly. For a very long time to come, however, the image of the Third World press in the developed world will continue to be coloured by the examples of President Marcos's Filipino press, operating under martial law to promote his particular brand of personal guidance of the nation, and President Suharto's press in Indonesia, which was simply closed down by government order at the time of the 1978 elections.

The concept of press freedom contains its paradoxes at the best of times. The reporter or editor who, in New York or London, claims that he may write exactly what he wishes is deceiving himself or his audience. There are limits to what a journalist at any moment may actually write, but the real and more powerful limits concern what he wishes to write. The forces in a society which govern the prevailing sense of plausibility, the instinct for what is salient, the feeling of what is relevant for the readers or listeners or viewers on a given day are the real mechanisms by which journalism in a society is controlled. The machinery is not necessarily one of censorship nor of self-censorship; it is something built into the professional training and the mores of the articulate in a given society. A sophisticated society controls its internal flows of information in ways more subtle than any government can duplicate or any legislature formulate. The ways in which information passes through a society are the key to that society's culture and are inseparable from its understanding of how to preserve itself and its internal group relationships. It is the silences that control a society and keep it 'stable' much more than the conscious noise which it generates.

The media of the nineteenth and twentieth centuries have turned themselves in the West into media which inform but which also in a sense control. At the time of Watergate one saw groups of journalists joining forces with the courts and the bureaucracy to eliminate a national leader who had gone out of control; the open system of American journalism makes it possible to leak as well as to publish.

Journalism is part of the mechanism of change. Once the investigative task was complete and the Nixon regime dismantled a rather different mood began to creep over the American press and the American courts. There is now as much an emphasis on the rights of citizens, companies, authorities to privacy as there is on the right of the press to expose. American society has gently reversed the euphoric aftermath of the 'investigative era' in journalism which reached its peak in the closing stages of the Vietnam War. The press doctrine of the West is not a God-given eternal doctrine, but an ever-shifting one, which ascribes rights and duties to different agencies in different historical contexts. The concepts of objectivity and impartiality are also heavily loaded with temporary meanings which constantly change emphasis. The dilemmas which beset Western journalism are at least as profound as those which appear more striking in the developing world between guided and free journalism, developmental and confrontational.

One has, therefore, in looking at the flow of opinion within the developing world, to realize that its press is a transplantation and a recent one at that; one must expect a transplanted journalism to contain, at least the range of problems and uncertainties which are contained within the original plant, plus a number of new ones. It is impossible even to scan the press of the Third World without constantly realizing the facts of dependence. The very technology of the media of the developing world illustrates the quest of the industrial nations to export their technology. The educational system of the industrial world and the whole of its culture are fashioned for expansion outwards from its metropolitan centres into whatever social vacuum can be found.

Western attitudes have been fed into the training of Third World journalists as much as that of other Third World technicians, professionals and craftsmen; inevitably, developing societies first imported an attempted Western newspaper culture when they imported the technology. The reporters of the developing world—those who have been trained abroad as well as those whose training has been on the newspapers in their own societies—tend to be judged by Western standards. There is no measure of competence which is separable from the beliefs and attitudes of those who have designed the standards. The whole professionalization of the media in developing countries is the result of cultural transplantation, and the practitioners have thus to struggle with the special contradictions of their situation.

Moreover, the institutions which have been built up in the receiving countries to house and energize the new technology are different in form from those from which the technology sprang. In certain societies, such as South America, the new media organizations follow the general pattern of branch-plant economies with the added complexity of close local governmental supervision. In most societies, however, newspaper and broadcasting organizations are directly governmental and the practitioners consider themselves employees of government. Though to Westerners they seem to be practising a form of journalism under 'occupation', their position makes them cohere much more to the local civil service than to the core professional loyalties which they may have been taught about in American or European journalism schools. In the developing world, the journalist frequently comes much closer to the heart of the contradictions of professionalism which are part and parcel of Western journalism.

It is not fully accepted in the West that journalism is a profession. The key criteria of professionalization are missing: collective control over entry to the group; a code of altruistic service, supported by scrupulous self-policing; a special set of skills based on the absorption of a definable body of knowledge and a set of 'client-type' relationships with the public. Journalism often lays claim to a form of professionalism while failing to comply with the crucial defining criteria. In the developing world, where the pressures on each individual are quite different and where salaries are in any case paid from the public purse, the para-professional code of Western journalism is very hard to adhere to. As they attempt to hold fast to the Western tradition of journalism, journalists in the developing world have a *much* harder time and are driven to more frequent compromises, without any supportive audience of colleagues. As Katz and Wedell point out,[2] broadcasting, in its transplanted context, continues to encompass the same repertoire of images of the listening public as in the originating countries of France and Britain. The idea of broadcasting as a continuous flow, and of its audience as a homogeneous family-based national unit, have been imported along with the structures of the BBC and the ORTF and the practitioners therefore wrestle with the task of pursuing irrelevant and unsuitable goals, their training for the task being only the precepts of a distant notional professionalism.

It is not surprising that many Asians and Africans, in particular, have become quickly disillusioned with the role of the journalist and have, perhaps reluctantly, come to reject 'professionalism' as an unworthy and self-preening device of Western reporters to maintain their social status within their own societies. Neville Jayaweera,[3] for example:

> The last thing media people can do is to come alive to the historical processes in which they are inextricably caught up and adapt their styles and priorities within them. Theirs has always been and will continue to be only a supportive role—supportive of values and systems that are not theirs to prescribe. Those values and systems are fashioned by economic and social forces much larger and more fundamental than themselves. The media ego must learn to diminish gracefully.

One theorist, Shelton A. Gunaratne,[4] argues that developmental journalism has something positive to offer as a substitute for Western professionalism and the inappropriate, inapplicable libertarian tradition which it carries with it. He sees a new journalism of the Third World operating in the 'social responsibility' tradition, the fourth of the 'Four Theories of Journalism' ('libertarian', 'communist', 'authoritarian' are the first three) that are described in Siebert, Peterson and Schramm's now classic essay.[5] This new trend involves 'analytic interpretation, subtle investigation, constructive criticism and sincere association with the grass roots, rather than with the elite'. One can see the logical evolution of the precepts involved in this 'new journalism', although it is difficult to find it practised very widely in the three great continents of the developing world. Gunaratne, however, makes a very effective case for debunking the 'subservience' of the Third World press, more widely practised and less often acknowledged. Media, either print or electronic, which are cajoled into a subservient role end up printing boastful government statements and compliantly announcing official plans without later pointing out when they fail to materialize. The developmental schools of journalism often slip into outright corruption and self-destructive 'self-regulation'. In the Philippine system it is forbidden for the press to criticize Marcos or his family or the military, while reflecting the goals of the New Society. The Indonesian media seem bound to follow the national ideology of 'Pancasila', while in Malaysia the media, fearful of the 1971 additions to the Sedition Ordinance, are forbidden to raise such matters as the language policy of the government, the special rights given to the Malay population, the role of the sultans and the citizenship policy for the non-

Malays; a long, bloody history of communal rioting lies behind the ordinance but it is difficult for a press to acquire any kind of self-confidence if it is prevented—in the name of 'Rukunegara', the national ideology—from dealing with the basic vexations of the society. The sadness of the situation of the press in many of the developing societies lies in the fact that its journalists, unable to reach out for their potential, really lead wasted lives. The professional training of the West has led to a widening of the gap between desire and opportunity without offering them a realizable set of goals, which a newer generation of Asian and African journalists are now painfully beginning to work out for themselves.

Peter Golding has itemized the failings of alien professional training.[6] It breeds 'internal emigrés' who cannot come to terms with the difficulties of their own societies. It lures staff away from their own media where they are needed, while they travel to a foreign place of training; here they are often deeply tempted to stay, adding to the professional brain drain experienced by Third World societies in so many other fields. Golding quotes from a report written by two African broadcasters after overseas attachments: 'It certainly looks good on the credit side of the aid ledger but in most cases the benefits derived by the recipient country do not justify the time spent on the attachment. . . . Usually African broadcasters going on attachments . . . either have to spend long periods learning a foreign language or return home after a tour of near mute observation. . . .'[7] Third World journalism has become over-attracted to empty 'qualifications' which do not actually help the recipient to perform the tasks concerned; there are predatory correspondence schools anxious to exploit the pining for occupational tags and labels, appealing to a misguided social spiralism.

The Western journalistic code arrives in Third World countries as a glamourized interposed set of ideals. Where the credibility of local media is weak, at least in comparison with the imported journals, radio signals and television programmes from Britain, France and America, inevitably the superiority of the import is ascribed to its superior professionalism—something which it proclaims constantly itself. An African or Asian journalist may try to see the problems of his own society and his own skill in other terms and, like very many, try to adopt a committed, not necessarily subservient, attitude to reporting his own society. But the flow of news from outside, upon which all the media of that society depends, cannot fail to influence. The result is an imposed veneer of foreign professional values, the adoption of which helps the individual in his career, while confusing his goals (a case of 'ideological convergence', as Peter Golding calls it). This is extremely painful for the journalist who is simply unable to observe the rules of professional autonomy and separateness from the state which the imported code harps upon.

All the tensions between public audience and professional provider in advanced industrialized societies are reversed in the case of the receiving societies. Urban élites, whose very existence is partly a distortion of developmental economics, demand sophisticated devices comparable with those of the emulated Western population. These devices (including television) have been produced in a special form to suit the prosperous mass market of a developed society and the technology required for manufacture is subject to patents and investments which systematically reinforce the supply and employment patterns of the advanced countries as well as the patterns of audience development. The kinds of professionalism which the Western media have developed—in print as well as electronic media—are predicated upon the need to maximize the attention of the entire society, which is fully literate, fully cognizant of a very broad inherited area of common allusion. The media professionalism of the 'First World' is separate from the society, alienated from it in many ways, constantly searching for points of mutuality where it can humanize itself and broaden its appeal. The importation of this whole apparatus of assumptions (riddled, it must be emphasized, with its own peculiar deficiencies, even in its own context) into the Third World merely helps to broaden the gap between its élites and its masses; where the media in the developed world act to homogenize society, in the Third World they divide, making the task of finding points of convergence between the leaders of the new nations and their subjects far more difficult. Of course, for well over a decade now, the search has shifted to the 'grassroots' and to new kinds of community leaders able to act as reporter, 'animateur', and broadcaster; but the whole nature of the technology itself makes the switch more rather than less difficult to achieve. Thus Nigeria has embarked upon colour television, while intermediate technology is still felt to be experimental and the likelihood is that the latest cheap, reliable and easily accessible technology will only spread deep into the Third World after it has become familiar as a toy in the West.

During the 1970s there were many examples of countries passing from free to controlled newspaper systems, and back again. India lost her free press during the period of Mrs Gandhi's emergency and then regained it. Spain, Greece and Portugal re-emerged from periods of dictatorship and newspaper repression. Chile slipped under the heel of a vicious censorship, while Brazil seemed to be moving very slowly, almost imperceptibly towards a loosening of controls by its military regime. Uganda, the Central African Empire, Nigeria and Ghana moved towards tighter and then lighter controls over the flow of information. The fact that these events occurred during a period when increased importance was being ascribed in international discussion to the role of information flow within societies meant that a great deal of active scrutiny was taking place. The shifts in both directions have produced, as it were, a body of laboratory data. It is possible to note trends over whole continents.

One may cite the example of Latin America, which began the post-war period with a wave of military dictatorships sweeping across the continent. The brief prosperity and liberalism of the 1940s, largely produced by the advantageous and collective balance of payments surpluses created during the Second World War, disappeared beneath the waves of dictatorship: Batista, Trujillo, Somoza, Jimenez, Peron either gained power or strengthened their grip over their respective nations, and the jails housed many of the most prominent editors and journalists of the continent. But the 1960s saw a reverse of the tide and a number of experiments in press freedom started up as the great dictators slipped from power. Only in Brazil did the trend work in reverse with the arrival of the military regime of 1964. By the end of the decade, however, Panama and Peru were subject to military coups and the model of the Cuban revolution became attractive to many in Latin America who saw Castro's brand of autocracy as a real path towards development. During the 1970s, the military had gradually taken over in Bolivia, Ecuador, Argentina, Chile, Uruguay, etc., etc. But in this most recent wave it is possible to discern a rather different attitude towards the press, in which a new set of methods—or at least a new terminology—has been adopted for the control of the press. The Peruvian regime announced in 1974 that newspapers had been seized in order to hand them over to 'organized sections of the population'. A few years later a new constitution was being prepared, including possibly a return of Lima's press to its former owners.

The Brazilian regime, in its post-1964 system, expressly guarantees the free expression of opinion and prohibits the censorship of newspapers; however, a series of special laws have set up a system of prior censorship which clearly overrides or modifies the constitutional principles. Journalists are forbidden, for example, to print 'classified information', the definition of which is left to the relevant authorities and is never made clear to the editors and reporters concerned. It is forbidden in Brazil, as in other countries, to create mistrust in the banking system and there is a law governing national security which prevents the circulation, even through true facts (which are claimed to be 'incomplete or distorted'), of information which spreads lack of confidence in the authorities. An arbitrariness thus governs the Brazilian press. Since a set of notional civil rights exists side by side with the more draconian laws, authorities are able to blow hot and cold as it suits them, and journalists who prepare carefully can often get interesting material past which is of direct political interest to the people of Brazil, especially if it is written in terms of the social and economic affairs of other countries. It has meant that there has been scope for skilful mutual handling by journalists and authorities, while a severe and repressive political system has persisted. Brazil now seems to be inching its way towards the end of the military government, but it is impossible to say how long the process will take or even whether it will go all the way.

The examples from Latin America show how varied the tools of press control have become and how much subtler than before is the current wave of international discussion of press freedom. The 1970s were very different from the Nazi days of press control and the newspaper repressions of the Third World are different in style, and perhaps intention too, from the systems of control built up in the 1950s in the countries of Eastern Europe, where an apparatus of such complete control was created that journalism there has in a sense now lost its will to change; only total upheavals, such as that of the Prague Spring, seem to offer any promise of change, and even then hardly within the existing political system.

There can be little doubt that the emergence of an accepted doctrine of developmental journalism has provided alibis and plausible excuses for regimes which have turned from open government to stringent repression. The doctrine can be used to provide 'cover', and its central principle easily turned to an empty rhetoric. Into this category falls the remarkable and well-documented twenty-month period of Mrs Gandhi's emergency in India. Because India was among the first of the Third World nations to develop an independence movement, it acquired a free press, or at least a press aspiring to be free on the European model, as far back as the 1870s. Indeed, the *Calcutta Journal*, the newspaper founded in 1818 by

James Silk Buckingham, one of the fathers of the modern Indian press and an early advocate of the political rights of Indians, declared its editor's duties as being 'to admonish governors of their duties, to warn them furiously of their faults and to tell disagreeable truths'.[8] During the colonial era, Indian editors acquired the double duty of keeping their readers informed of the activities of the British authorities while attempting to get information from India through to the Parliament and government of Britain. Very frequently the local authorities saw their function as that of controlling the flow of information in both directions. When, in 1910, the Indian News Agency, which had always had difficulties in keeping itself financially afloat, was merged with Reuters, a period of great difficulty was inaugurated for Indian editors. Even when, in 1930, Reuters became a trust owned by 190 British newspapers and dedicated to the un-coloured presentation of objective truth, it was found wanting in respect of its role within India since it was subject to powerful influences both in London and Delhi, especially at times of political crisis. The 1954 Report of the Press Commission in India declares that in the 1920s both Reuters and the Associated Press of India (started by the Anglo-Indian papers and later also merged with Reuters) attempted to hamper the flow of news concerning the non-co-operation movement and the civil disobedience passing from India to London.[9] Indian political and economic leaders felt that their views were not being communicated to London. India's struggle for independence was greatly complicated by the problems of its own élite in dealing with the British authorities. In fact, the Vernacular Press Act of 1878 had been directly aimed at holding back the new generation of Indian indigenous journalists. Indian independence thus has its roots in the same soil as European nationalism, although acquiring very early a character of its own.

When India finally did achieve independence she had already acquired a sophisticated press, experienced in agitation, but also knowledgeable in the arts of government. It played an important part in the creation of the image of the new national leaders. It saw their victory as its victory and in the 1950s it did not pursue any form of confrontation with its new rulers. Only when new divisions became clear in the 1960s between a purely Indian bourgeoisie and a more radical alternative did the Indian press begin to acquire the adversary role which so angered Mrs Gandhi after the splitting of the Congress Party in 1969. One group of newspapers, the more powerful at that, broke with her and disagreed with her policies on such matters as the dispossession of the former Indian princes and the taking over of the banking system.

However, it has to be pointed out that the press in India, during periods of co-operation, subservience and repression, as well as during its more recalcitrant and oppositional periods, has never been a mass medium; it has always circulated among the inter-connected grouping of landowners, industrialists, bureaucrats, industrial executives and politician-intellectuals which constitutes the Indian élite. The 'real' processes of communication within Indian society take place at village level among a non-literate population. The rural masses have a personal traditional communication system which has not yet been deeply affected by the advent of modern media. Indeed, the media themselves form one of the boundary lines between the educated urban élite and the rural population. Regional, linguistic and ethnic differences divide the non-urban population. The divisions of geography do not in themselves serve as the boundaries of the myriad cultures of India. There are 800 dialects and fourteen major languages and no single indigenous language is shared even by the élite. The role of Hindi as a national language is still hotly disputed, leaving English, the language of the hated colonialists, as the only common medium of discourse, which today acts if anything as a further complicating frontier between élite and rural masses. Gandhi had tried to create a new national language out of a combination of Urdu and Hindi which he himself spoke, known as Hindustani. In his mouth it was a moving and eloquent medium, with which he could rouse hundreds of thousands of people, but the effort to establish it has not survived him.

The Indian intelligentsia has, therefore, found itself internally divided between adherence to the interconnected social and business élite and rejection of it, without having physical or linguistic means of constructing for themselves an alternative base of operation. Even within the government there is a division between those who want to advance towards socialism—on an Indian pattern—and those who see the future only in terms of further importations of Western institutions and techniques. India is a country with an intellectual élite which is perhaps further alienated from its own masses than that of any other developing society. Even where the progress of national development provides an opportunity for mass media to develop (e.g., in the medium of film), the support of most of the intellectual élite for 'modernization' has served to separate them from their own masses. Tens of thousands of talented and trained

Indians pass to and from the Western industrialized societies acquiring more and more 'training' and 'professionalism' but returning to India to eschew the traditional culture with its wealth of allusion and folk arts, which are simply relegated to a status of permanent 'primitivism'.

The 'professional' media occupy a disproportionate share of the media resources without finding a way to reach the Indian masses. The suggestion that the intellectual élite should master the traditional techniques of communication would be seen as a lowering of 'standards', a betrayal of 'excellence', so deeply rooted are the attitudes and perceptions of Western training models. Throughout rural India, a layer of local business and political officials and entrepreneurs helps to entrench the separation of intelligentsia from the masses. Kusum Singh describes the problems even in radio of providing a flow of information from town to village:

> ... Even community radio sets have not radically changed the information flow because the government radio is usually in the courtyard of a member of the *panchayat* (village council). News travels faster but the rural elite are the first to have it. ... The mass media can do little unless 'hooked into' that interpersonal network that enables people to bypass the traditional rural elite.[10]

The cynicism and distrust felt by both sides of the divide about the other have been compounded by the failure of the ideals and programmes of the last thirty years to work. There has been little progress either towards equality or world economic growth and the long-term failure has created a kind of stubborn opposition or indifference towards the ideals themselves. The idea of a 'developmental' ethic arrived rather early in Indian thinking about the role of the mass media outside the cities; a society in a process of change, it was thought, ought to emphasize the responsibilities among the professionals of the media. Indian radio, television and print have come to shape their messages according to the view of the authorities on how to implement the nation's goals. The media, even where privately owned, have acquired a strong streak of bureaucratic thought, detectable in the English-language media as well as the vernacular. Unwritten self-censorship principles have been adopted almost unconsciously and the injustices and corruption of the society proceed without comment. Indeed, one prominent editor said to the present author that 'corruption' as such would not be perceived as a major 'story' to an Indian journalist.

In radio and the press, senior staff, although highly trained and professional in a Western sense, create a kind of double standard for themselves. Where they are communicating within the élite they perceive the direct relevance of the Western media models through which they have been trained (and to which many of them have in fact made important contributions); but in looking at the rest of their own society they perceive an overriding compulsion towards other standards. Creative staff switch from the role of autonomous intellectual to that of bureaucrat as they switch audience. It seems natural to take orders from above when preparing the content of a medium designed to reach the rural population, an audience which seems necessarily subject to the prescribed goals of government. Thus, Indian radio, with its extraordinarily varied audiences, is controlled ultimately by a professional élite of broadcasters, with a single national news service. The bureaucracy of the provinces is constantly pitted against that of Delhi. Of course, there have been in the last decade tens of thousands of villages reached via satellite and as many again provided with local interactive community radio, but this movement has not penetrated the bulk of the half billion people of India. Even the film industry, of which the output is enormous (the largest national film industry in the world, in fact), reaches only a small section of the ex-urban masses. India's films are distributed through less than 10,000 outlets, including the touring cinemas. Educational and informational films are shown alongside the popular musical offerings of the commercial industry and the government has created a public sector industry to provide them, but no organization exists to bring this material to the hundreds of thousands of remote villages. In any case, very little of India's tremendous cinematic output brings home to the audience the appalling facts of Indian life, its poverty and deprivation, its oppression and pointless inequalities.[11]

India is perhaps the best example of the way in which modernization has amounted to the thoughtless transplantation of institutions, practices, standards, along with only partially relevant technologies. In fact, the process of transplantation in India has succeeded to the point at which it is self-generating and self-perpetuating, enlarging the urban élite upon which it grows and exacerbating those social divisions which information could be attempting to diminish. The birth control programme which was the most memorable aspect of Mrs Gandhi's twenty-month emergency and which was one main cause of her downfall, was the classic product of a media 'transplant' situation. The goals of the programme were bureaucratically conceived and technologically executed; the rural population were subjected to it rather than offered it or, still less, consulted about it. Underlying the whole programme was the assumption that the media professionals and their masters, the bureaucrats and politicians, had only to activate the masses to accept the technology which was offered them and that nothing further needed to be learned by the élite from the people who were the objects of their attention. And yet to the people responsible for the birth control programme it seemed that the Indian villages lay in the grip of an impenetrable ignorance and traditionalism, which could be reversed only through exhortation backed by force, in order that India could be thrust into the next necessary stage of its development. Kusum Singh singles out the 'relentless bureaucratic culture' as in a sense the clue to the problem of cultural domination in India:

> They [the media intellectuals] are caught between the conflicting pull of the formal ritualism of the past and the rationalistic methods of the future, resulting in a paralysis of creativity. The media professionals themselves complain that some of the best minds in the country are worn out by administrative and organizational chores, leaving no time or energy for creative work . . . craving of government recognition is deeply rooted in most intellectuals.[12]

Even before the emergency was declared the relationship between the Delhi government and the press, and between the state governments and the press was clearly passing through a new and unfamiliar stage. Roughly, three-quarters of all the advertising carried in Indian newspapers originates in an institution controlled by government, and Delhi exercises other important powers through the Indian state monopoly over the importing and distribution of newsprint (greatly strengthened in the 1970s with the tremendous increase in the international price of newsprint). An attempt by the government to control the total amount of newsprint which a single newspaper could consume was ruled unconstitutional by the Supreme Court in 1973. The Press Council of India, meanwhile, feeling that tensions with the government were increasing, set about strengthening the freedoms of editors, sometimes in the teeth of opposition by state governments. The press was feeling confident to launch a number of attacks on the apparently increasing corruption within the administration and to attack the government's failures in the economy, when suddenly Mrs Gandhi struck out in June 1975 and declared the state of emergency. In order to stop the news of mass arrests spreading around the country in the immediate aftermath, the authorities had taken the shrewd precaution of switching off the electricity supply to Delhi newspapers, so that the news of the emergency could not be printed until the censorship system was working.

Mrs Gandhi's censorship employed the full range of euphemisms familiar to all students of dictatorships since the eighteenth century. It prohibited anything denigrating the office of prime minister, or that might bring the legal government into hatred or contempt, or 'that might promote feelings of enmity or hatred between different classes of citizens', or might cause the 'cessation and slowing down of work'. The decree speaks of preventing demoralization, 'worsening of the law and order situation', 'disaffection between the government and the people'. The reporting of Parliament and of law courts was expressly forbidden prior to government vetting.

Across India the censorship operated in different ways, in some states with censors sitting in editorial offices, in others with a total pre-censorship on all news. In some places a kind of self-censorship was instituted. All were encouraged to perform their duty through the frequent arrests of journalists, closures of papers and a repertoire of petty harassments. The Press Council was abolished. The immunity to prosecution granted to newspapers in connection with the reporting of Parliament was repealed. The Prevention of Publication of Objectionable Matters Act was made a constitutional provision to prevent it being challenged in the courts. The four news agencies of India were merged 'voluntarily' into one state puppet, Samachar, which was used in furtherance of the censorship to bring about positive as well as negative control of newspaper content. Under the chairmanship of the chief censor a group of editors was brought together to draw up a 'code of editorial ethics'. Of India's 17,064 newspapers and periodicals, 1,100 had the benefit of governmental advertising restricted or removed.

The *Statesman*, one of the most important newspapers of India, was systematically deprived of governmental advertising and an attempt was made to cajole the shareholders into selling out. The *Express* was subjected to a complex of harassments: electricity was cut off, false allegations about infringements of the law were made; the banks were prevented from co-operating with it; its publisher and his family were threatened with jail on trumped-up charges; its advertising was removed. It survived after an initial weakening, partly with the help of the courts. Needless to say, many more newspapers, under weaker management or under crushing administrative blows, collapsed morally and became tools of the emergency government. The courts made a number of important and telling points against the role and practice of the chief censor, such as when the government attempted to stop the High Court from publishing its own judgement on a case which the government wished to appeal to the Supreme Court. 'The censor is not above the court,' declared the court. 'It is necessary for him to realize that he is subject to the jurisdiction of the court. What is held *ultra vires* cannot be allowed to operate as *intra-vires* under the veil of secrecy.'[13] Newspapers which went ahead and published the court judgements fell victim to harassment. Of course, all the other media of the country, which, unlike the press, are directly controlled by government, were turned into propagandistic mouthpieces.

When Mrs Gandhi decided to call an election in February 1977, the censorship was relaxed (not ended). A great upsurge took place almost spontaneously in the direct coverage of events; circulations of those papers which had resisted the administrative measures shot up and that of collaborationist papers wasted away. Press freedom became a major issue in the election itself and the Congress Party, the only party left supporting censorship as being in the national interest, was ousted.

Outside the communist world, no similarly comprehensive attempt at massive newspaper censorship has been attempted in a country with so deeply rooted a tradition of press freedom and so large a journalistic community as India. It was evidently extremely difficult for the Indian government to maintain the kind of detailed control it wanted over an industry which was in private ownership; it was attempting the kind of controls that are only possible when state, governing party and newspaper plants are all under unitary line control and management, and this was at no time the case with the Indian newspaper industry under the emergency. India presents the example of a European free press planted in an Asian society with which it is not in complete consonance; the troubles of Mrs Gandhi in attempting to control it bring out some of the real problems which beset it.

In 1978 India, now under the decentralist Janata Government, set up a new Press Council with the object 'to preserve the freedom of the press and to maintain and improve the standards of newspapers and news agencies in India.'[14] Paradoxically, its powers and functions are set out in an act of Parliament. The Press Council will in due course produce an amended code of conduct for newspapers and journalists and help to build up the sense of responsibility and public service of newspaper practitioners. It monitors the performance of the press and scrutinizes the relations between government and the press as well as the general economic condition of the industry. It examines such problems as concentration of ownership and internal relationships between reporters, editors and publishers or owners. Its powers are ultimately to censure editors who misbehave and oblige newspapers to publish its adjudications, which may not cover any matters about which any proceeding is pending in a court of law. Its powers are to summon individuals to attend its hearings, examine them upon oath, insist on the production of relevant documents (including public records). No editor or journalist may be compelled, however, to reveal the sources of any information received or reported. It is precisely the kind of statutory body which the United Kingdom has striven to avoid, as have other countries in Europe, although several have acquired press councils with similar or weaker powers, operating non-statutorily, like the British Press Council and the National News Council of the United States.

A series of important initiatives, closely observed by the rest of the developing world, has been taken in the aftermath of the emergency in India, in addition to the reconstitution of the Press Council. Historically, India has enjoyed a widely accessible popular culture which spreads an acquaintance with traditions even to the remotest parts of the sub-continent. Travelling bards and folk-singers traversed the entire country. The great epics like *Ramayana* and *Mahabharata* were the possession of the entire society and even in the present century the most successful communicators in India have not been those who have acquired Western 'professionalism' but others who have based their appeal and their methods upon the traditional networks. Gandhi published his writings in magazines with a total print order of 40,000, yet attracted hundreds of millions of people to his person and his ideas.

Since independence, despite the growth of railways, canals, roads, airlines, radio and television, communication of new ideas has been hamstrung. Even though radio covers three-quarters of the country, there exist only 20 million radio receivers among the 600 million population. Of these, 5 million are shared by the 450 million villagers.

In Bihar, there is one receiver for 96 inhabitants. Despite the profusion of publications, less than 40 per cent of adult males can read and less than 20 per cent of females. A vast army of professionals would have to be created if the media or modern civilization were to continue to develop in their current forms.[15] There is no way in which 600,000 villages can be equipped with a full range of modern print and electronic media, and experiments with satellite communication in recent years have only made evident the enormity of the terrestrial task of creating material comprehensible to a nation with such variations of language and culture.[16] Each of India's four National Plans has come a little closer to acknowledging the importance of rural communication and the 'essential human inputs' which Indian communication requires. In the aftermath of the emergency a large-scale adult literacy programme has been launched which should in itself provide for the constant expansion of the printed word, even though it will do little to change the social *structure* of Indian illiteracy. Only a vast movement from the bottom upwards could begin to do that, but the government of India is far from being able to bring such a phenomenon about.

The gaps in India's media are glaring. Of the 500 commercial films made annually, almost none is dedicated to a basic social purpose. The technicians and directors have not been trained to perform such tasks. The public sector film industry produces 140 documentaries and over a hundred newsreels every year—which are seen by about 70 million people a year, most of them in the cities. If the field-cinemas continued in perpetual motion for ten years there are enough to reach every village in India once in a decade. The Film and Television Institute of India is now attempting to establish some form of direct contact in order to stimulate interest in the content of the films; most of the officers concerned are completely untrained for the work, which is in any case very typical of the 'trickle down' policies of Indian communication. Floods and cyclones contribute greatly to the tragedies of Indian communication planning. On paper there exist some tens of thousands of group listening communities, pioneered by the Rural Forum Scheme in Poona some years ago; they are thought to be listening to special radio programmes which they then discuss and act upon, but nobody is certain how many are active since there is no staff constantly monitoring them. A host of other community services by radio has been inaugurated, including teacher-training projects and school broadcasts, but all of this panoply of activity flows outwards from a single organization, All

India Radio (AIR), which can scarcely conduct the necessary monitoring of projects in hundreds of dialects and languages.

The television service (Doordashan), which dates back to a UNESCO project of 1956, reveals these patterns even more woefully: there are now 17 stations covering about 7 per cent of the area and 16 per cent of the population. After several years of development, only 67,000 receivers exist in the cities of India and about 5,000 scattered rural communal receivers among hundreds of thousands of villages.[17]

As in the industrialized world, very little reliable information exists concerning the educational impact of television or how best to fit it into an examination-oriented educational system. Nonetheless, since the SITE experiment a great deal of further work has been done in India in the use of television in primary school teaching, with tens of thousands of teachers involved in the projects.

It is easy to castigate the pitiful progress of India towards providing its population with information adequate to its urgent needs. It is perhaps equally important to register the clear lessons which were learned during the emergency. Radio and television have been subject to a commission under the leadership of George Verghese (formerly Editor of the *Hindustan Times*), which recommended a greatly enhanced independence for All India Radio and Doordashan; it also recommended a system of 'franchise stations', low-power transmitters operating in universities and technical institutions and under local control. The proposals have been considerably watered down as a government with little experience in large-scale decentralization and very chary of releasing its grip over matters which have traditionally fallen within the purview of central government has attempted to experiment with media independence. It is also important to give credit to the overall feedback from the SITE experiment, which is now known to have reached 200,000 villagers every day during its months of operation in 1975. Doordashan learned a great deal from its experience in making hundreds of hours of television programmes on one inch and half-inch video tape. SITE did not fall, despite predictions that it would, into the trap of mass entertainment; it remained an educational project and was not tempted to comply with exported assumptions about television derived from Western experience. There has been some evidence that the innovations in agriculture, hygiene and health have in fact been adopted permanently in some of the villages, but a lack of follow-up investigation denies us any real certainty.

This brief account of the dilemmas of the Indian media—or some of them—shows how difficult it is to get beyond the perception of the need for some new synthesis of journalistic values into the practice of a new 'developmental' journalism. India cannot clearly formulate its new needs because of the social system in which its media practitioners are captured, and because of the social blinkers which they are obliged to wear, irrespective of the interference by government in the content of a wide range of media. The subjection of India to foreign dominant models for its media institutions and practices has deprived it of that clarity of purpose which is the very thing it needs to gain some control over the intractable problems of size and diversity. The emergency was an aberration which revealed the inadequacies of the preceding situation, even though this derived from perhaps the best traditions of the European press. Today India might be tempted towards more daring governmental policies, but 'policies' they will be, never permitted to fall from the grip of government. The position of other developing societies is, of course, a good deal worse than India's, with its long journalistic tradition.

The closer one attempts to focus upon the communication problems of another society the greater the dilemma over the assessment of cause and effect becomes. There is an obvious connection between economic development and the provision of communications and it is almost impossible to perceive which is the active stimulant of the other, although it seems clear that distortions and dependences in one area will lead to comparable patterns in the other. In the UN's first Development Decade of the 1960s there was considerable optimism that the spread of communications media would produce the breakthrough in economic development, but it was gradually and bitterly discovered that provision was only the starting-point; the socialization of the media, its equipment, and the recruitment and training of workers and managers were much more intractable problems and tended to multiply the very confusions of the receiving society that had led to its 'backwardness'. In the 1970s the media was regraded downwards as a source of dynamic change. It has taken further years to realize that the media can, if circumstances are right and preparation undergone with care, play an extremely important role in triggering the will to develop and in helping societies prepare themselves for 'take-off' from traditional to modern. Great emphasis is placed today on the importance of face-to-face communication in the tasks of teaching hygiene, birth control, agricultural techniques.

At the same time that the power of communications media was being questioned by development experts, communications experts were questioning the accepted notions of development. One group of specialists were thus asking how to engineer the gaps between knowledge, attitude and practice while the other were asking more insidious questions such as how the ownership and control of the media in developing societies could be affecting their acceptability and whether the media of given societies were doing little more than serve the moral interests of one section of a community which was being systematically provided with an inadequate view of the world.

It was at this point—perhaps at the start of the 1970s—that an important group of communications researchers within the developing world came to present their own ideas, which resolved some of the previous doubts. It became clear—very quickly it seemed —that there were alien models for media institutions which did not apply to societies other than the ones which had originally acquired them for their own historical reasons. Furthermore, there was a linkage between political, economic and communications considerations which had to be resolved within each society for itself. Mere technology would do nothing except transplant further distorting machinery to the receiving country. Throughout the world in the 1970s there was the spread of a search for new communication models and adaptable institutions; it affected the thinking of the industrialized world with all of its certainties, as well as the developing continents. Each wave of repression in Third World countries and media left behind a sediment of realizations, the disillusionments being perhaps more enriching than was thought at the time.

Meanwhile, in all of the countries enjoying a 'free' press, in both the developed and the developing worlds, a great deal of soul-searching went on throughout the period after the tumultuous events of the year 1968. It became clear that there were enormous variations in media practice and that there were no general criteria of freedom to which any nation was obliged to adhere, merely a series of trade-offs which left some in a happier position than others. Suddenly there was a much greater range of institutional examples available for the Third World to borrow. It was possible to have a Swedish-style Ombudsman or Press Council. It was possible to have community involvement in the control of media, or even government ownership or public participation in shareholding without losing the general ideal of a press which served the interests of its society. Many Western societies found it necessary to make major intrusions into what was previously deemed to be an area of necessary freedom from law: laws sprang up all over Western Europe preventing discrimination in media against immigrant or minority groups, against women, against a great range of non-conformists. Newspapers and the media in general were shown to have been manipulating matters of public taste and even of political preference in countries claiming to enjoy a completely independent media system. The lines of responsibility and irresponsibility were being redrawn. UNESCO was already raising a comparable range of questions in the international field and opened the door for a new self-questioning among developing nations, which, however, has not always led them towards an opening-up of their media. As we have seen, the tide of freedom and openness in public media has ebbed and flowed, but it has resulted in a great deal of experimentation in the search for more appropriate doctrines.

Within the West there have been those who have decided that any questioning of the practices of the world agencies or of the major newspapers of the West can only be performed from a position of hostile autocracy. Certainly both agencies and major newspapers have their scars to display: throughout South America and Africa foreign newsmen have been tortured and harassed and nationals have been prevented from circulating information. But the 1980s look like being a decade of improvement in which the worst examples of the repression of the 1970s may be revealed for what they are, a self-destructive but conspicuous attempt by insecure ruling groups to retain their power.

Throughout this book it has been argued that the problems of the Third World's press have to a large extent been caused by the ways in which the economies of the North have used those of the South. Today the political power of the North has been rolled back, especially as a result of the American defeat in South-East Asia, and beneath the carpet of American power the whole world begins to look different. The South is still very far from being economically independent, but its collective political strength is sufficient to force different perspectives into a condition of plausibility. American information does not go unchallenged and the continuing needs of American technology in space and in the electro-magnetic spectrum mean that America and the West as a whole must make compromises and deals where previously the right of free flow was backed by a guarantee of delivery. It is very difficult for a civilization to have its values questioned, but that necessarily follows the questioning of its power.

The West has of course been pushed back rather than pushed out, and it remains the dominant force in the world; but it has now to come to terms with the fact that a vast sector of the world will no longer accept its values along with its technology and its investment. It has now to examine the evolving beliefs of others to see if something can be learned or adapted, for it is the superstructure of Western beliefs and values in the field of information which is principally in crisis.

Until the present, most Western commentators have chosen to equate developmental news with government-dominated news. In fact, the former requires the same faculty of critical examination, the same kind of investigative instinct as libertarian journalism. It should not be confused either with development support communication, which is designed directly to support and promote the cause of economic development, although in countries in which the media are directed by government a certain overlap inevitably occurs. Distinctions must also be drawn between those Third World leaders who simply declare that 'Western journalists should take their news straight from us' and those who really believe that government controls are necessary at a certain stage of development of their societies. Many supporters of the New International Information Order or those who are demanding the institution of a new obligatory code of conduct for foreign journalists are not in fact supporters of a government-controlled press at all. What these are aiming at is a real balance in the flow of understanding between North and South. It is hypocrisy, however, to claim that this would not interfere with a free flow, because it must do precisely that, for free flow is not ultimately reconcilable with a guaranteed balance.

Altaf Gauhar asks whether media truth is the same as truth. 'Truth means endless search, based on reflection, investigation, interpretation and discovery, and whether absolute or relative, truth has an independent existence. It does not depend for its emergence on deadlines. Nor does it have to be governed by the availability of space. The value of truth is not determined by its acceptability or plausibility.'[18] There has been in the past a powerful counter to the values of journalistic truth in the universities, but today they have, like much else, been dragged into the same categories.[19] Much academic research has come to aspire to the condition of news, instead of the other way around, and these two separate disciplines, both based upon roughly similar human purposes—the pursuit of credible and socially useful information—have come to overlap and, in a sense, compete. Within the West, journalism has become an increasing source of political and social power in the era of mass democracy and mass manipulative politics. Indeed, the *management* of journalism and journalists has become a primary technique of Western politicians, and all those who seek to gain the attention of · those politicians. The general crisis within Western journalism arises from the growing gulf between its theory and the constraints of markets, technology, institutions and situations within which it operates.

The attack by the Third World is, of course, part of a more general assault on the economy and power of the West. The response of the latter's information corporations and institutions has mainly been to mount a (largely successful) propaganda offensive and the battlefield of UNESCO has—perhaps to its surprise—been held by the West despite the frequency and variety of the manoeuvres. No one, however, expects the Third World pressures to diminish in the 1980s. The reverse is to be expected. What then should now be the approach of those in North and South who, broadly speaking, desire to preserve the notions and practices of classic journalistic freedom both from the fork-tongued criticism of certain Third World spokesmen and from its own failures to meet the needs of a more politically balanced globe? Basically, editors and publishers have to adjust themselves to the fact that their role within the marketplace of the Western readership and audience is now an internationally charged role. The entertainment of that audience entails the dissemination of stereotypes which have become a political danger in themselves. The newspaper and media empires of the West are a luxury of capital which perhaps it can no longer afford, in the sense that their profitability has been built, in part, upon journalistic practices and priorities which are open to severe charges but which have been long protected against significant criticism. The argument about the values and attitudes of journalism has to be carried through the whole world of practitioners in the hope of securing important changes in daily practice. It is precisely those who benefit from 'free flow' who are best able to make adjustments and it is only when the shockwaves of the current debate affect the whole internal structure of Western information that a new world-oriented journalism of the late twentieth century can be fashioned.

Conclusion

> Many people have come to realize that sovereignty, identity
> and independence result not only from formal political decisions
> but are also, and perhaps even more, contingent upon the conditions
> of cultural and economic life . . . in short, upon circumstances
> which affect, in an increasingly interlocking fashion, the overall
> development of each and every nation.

Among the mosaic of politically adroit statements and positions
of which the MacBride Commission is composed, that sentence
clearly offers a reasonable summary of the core problem. The cause
of the New International Information Order is strengthened by the
growing realization that information structures are in a sense pre-
determinants of the viability of nations. But the MacBride Report
has tried at the same moment to locate the problem somewhat
beyond reach of Mustapha Masmoudi's shrill demands, while
elevating the discussion and spreading the responsibility for the
problems of the moment to all governments, corporations and
bureaucracies which inhibit the free flow of knowledge. It rightly
shows how the world imbalance is made up to some extent of
obstructions and dislocations within nations and among nations of
the same bloc. 'Inequalities exist everywhere, in all societies, on all
levels, within countries and between countries and within and
between regions.'

The trouble is that a clever (but fair) restatement of the problem is
not tantamount to a resolution. Most of the practical suggestions
of the Report, although relevant and efficacious in themselves,
would not together actually add up to the elimination of imbalance
or inequality or obstructed flow. 'It is vital to endeavour obstinately
and patiently to reduce them.' Surely so, but the desire is seldom
father to the fact, and it is unlikely that attention will be paid by
those who are the most at fault. In any case, one cannot but be
struck by the fact that the problems are so deeply rooted in history
and in the geology of human attitudes that one cannot expect to
see a reversal of these inequalities without major shifts in world
power greater than those which have yet taken place.

This essay has taken a different—perhaps more pessimistic—line of
argument than MacBride. It has argued that the existing information

order of the world is a product of and has itself extended the historical relationships between the 'active' and the 'passive' civilizations, the seeing and the seen, imperial and empire, exploring and explored. The prosperous nations of the North have not come to terms with the fact that they are now being obliged to be themselves 'observed' as the relative political status of the great power blocs is beginning to change. They are insisting upon their cultural prowess, even where their economic and political power has been diminished; it is this which has suddenly made developing countries aware of how dependent they had been, causing them to seize upon the news flow issue as a method of taking control of their own world image—with some success.

A new group of agencies has sprung into activity determined to reverse the world's news imbalances, but the existing Western agencies are themselves beginning to alter the reflexes and procedures of international journalism in such a way as to redress some of the injustice without losing their grip upon the lion's share of international news. In any case, there is no chance that the Third World will generate a large volume of independently sold and internationally acceptable information about itself until more developing nations establish the principle of a free press which, again, is unlikely, despite certain recent hopeful signs. Perhaps the greatest weakness in the list of demands which makes up the New International Information Order has been its lack of conception of the primal value of press freedom (and of intellectual freedom as a whole). In a sense, the order was formulated by the wrong people in the wrong way, although much of the sentiment supporting them has been genuine and even in certain respects liberating; but seldom can the charter of a great political cause have been so mean in spirit, so ungenerous in sentiment, so obsessively petty, so insistent upon the obligations of others and so niggardly in ascribing difficult duties to its own adherents. Of course, many of its supporters have been Third World journalists deeply committed to the ideals of freedom. They have modified some of its documents and introduced more traditionally liberal concepts but they have not eradicated its fundamentally flawed inspiration. It is possible that with the deliberations of the World Administrative Radio Conference, the publication of the MacBride Report and the preparations for a new general conference of UNESCO, it will fade away and be replaced by something more fitting to be the cornerstone of an important political world movement.

Perhaps the most far-reaching anxiety which these pages have attempted to emphasize springs from the terrific investment now under way in the field of telecommunications. Preparations for a new industrial revolution on such a scale as that made necessary by the advent of the new micro-electronics and the new telecommunications systems should be conducted more with a view to its global implications than to the short-term interests of the transnational companies and quasi-monopolies which dominate these fields. This is an area for real international action, for without it the inequalities between world sectors could become irretrievably gross. Indeed, the threat to independence in the late twentieth century from the new electronics could be greater than was colonialism itself. We are beginning to learn that de-colonization and the growth of supra-nationalism were not the termination of imperial relationships but merely the extending of a geo-political web which has been spinning since the Renaissance. The new media have the power to penetrate more deeply into a 'receiving' culture than any previous manifestation of Western technology. The results could be immense havoc, an intensification of the social contradictions within developing societies today. In the West we have come to think of the 2,500 communication satellites which presently circle the earth as distributors of information. For many societies they may become pipettes through which the data which confers sovereignty upon a society is extracted for processing in some remote place.

Though there is little which can be done to reorder rapidly the gross imperfections of the world information system as it stands, it must surely be within the power of governments and in the long-term interest of corporations to see that the new networks are constructed in a spirit of real interdependence. This might involve making uncomfortable concessions to developing societies in the distribution of radio frequencies; it might entail obliging computer manufacturers to work in partnership with Third World governments. It would certainly involve the encouragement of linkages between manufacturing bases for equipment between developing societies. Though it is difficult to root out the imbalances which stem from the past, there is a sense in which the 'information society' anticipated for the 1980s and 1990s could deliberately be treated as the opportunity for a new beginning.

Notes

Preface

1. *Many Voices, One World*, the final report of the International Commission for the Study of Communication Problems (The MacBride Report) was published by UNESCO in Paris, in 1980. Its Interim Report was published in September 1978.
2. In particular as a result of the title of the French governmental report by Simon Nora and Alain Minc, 'L'Informatisation de la Société', La Documentation Française, Paris, 1978. English translation forthcoming from MIT Press, Boston, 1980.

Chapter 1

1. Hugh Clifford, *Further India*, Lawrence and Lullen Ltd, London, 1904, p. 5.
2. H. J. Wood, *Exploration and Discovery*, Hutchinson, London, 1951.
3. William Stevenson, *Historical Sketch of the Progress of Discovery, Navigation and Commerce from the Earliest Records to the Beginning of the Nineteenth Century*, William Blackwood, Edinburgh, 1824, *passim*.
4. John Livingstone Lowes, *The Road to Xanadu: A Study in the Ways of the Imagination*, Vintage Books, New York, 1959 edition (published originally in 1927), p. 111. Much of the information about these strange nations is also drawn from the second section of this work.
5. See Joseph Frank, *The Beginnings of the English Newspaper, 1620–1660*, Oxford University Press and Harvard University Press, 1961, for a detailed account of the evolution of the news controversy among English journalists of the Civil War.
6. *The Works of Lucian of Samosata* (translated by H. W. Fowler and F. G. Fowler), Vol. 2, Clarendon Press, Oxford, 1905, pp. 131–2.
7. Henry James, *The Reverberator*, Macmillan, New York, 1888.
8. Evelyn Waugh, *Scoop*, Chapman & Hall, London, 1938.
9. Rudyard Kipling, *The Light that Failed*, National Publishers, New York, 1890.
10. George Meredith, *Diana of the Crossways*, Chapman & Hall, London, 1885.
11. Clifford, op. cit., p. 1.
12. P. T. Moon, *Imperialism and World Politics*, Macmillan, New York, 1926, p. 66. Quoted by Phil Harris in 'News Dependence: The Case for a New World Information Order'. This was the final report to UNESCO of a study of the international news media, unpublished, University of Leicester, November 1977, p. 28.
13. Basil Davidson, *Africa in History: Themes and Outlines*, Paladin, London, 1974, p. 183.
14. Figures from Mustapha Masmoudi, 'The New World Information Order', in *Journal of Communication*, Vol. 29, No. 2, Spring 1979, p. 183 (but quoted from UN sources).
15. Ibid.
16. Clifford Geertz, *The Interpretation of Cultures*, Hutchinson, London, 1975, and Basic Books, New York, 1973, pp. 234–43.
17. This and the other quotations in this section are taken from the article by Mustapha Masmoudi cited in note 14 above, which is the locus classicus of the NIIO.

18. Okot p'Bitek, *The Song of Lawino and The Song of Ocol*, East African Publishing House, Nairobi, 1972, p. 54.
19. Ibid., p. 229.

Chapter 2

1. Tapio Varis, 'Global Traffic in Television', *Journal of Communication*, Vol. 24, 1974, pp. 102–9.
2. Kent Cooper, *Barriers Down*, Farrer and Rinehart, New York, 1942, p. 43.
3. See Chapter Two of Herbert Schiller, *Communications and Cultured Dominance*, M. E. Sharpe, Inc., New York, 1976, pp. 24–45 (originally published in *Le Monde Diplomatique*, September 1975).
4. The figures in this paragraph are drawn from *Advertising Age* for 29 March 1976, and from other tables published in Jeremy Tunstall, *The Media are American*, Constable, London, 1977, pp. 294–5.
5. UNESCO figures.
6. Japan Newspaper Publishers' Association (NSK) figures.
7. See 'A Glimpse into Communications Statistics', Research Paper No. 6 of the International Commission for the Study of Communication Problems, p. 5.
8. Figures calculated by *Television Radio Age International*, September 1979, and based on statistics from the UN and from individual countries.
9. Gail M. Martin and Jean McNulty, 'Communication Policy in Canada. Telecommunications Research Group, unpublished, Simon Fraser University, Burnaby, BC, January, 1979.
10. See article by Bernard Ostry, Deputy Minister of Communications of Canada, 'Telecommunications in Canada: Today, Tomorrow and Next Week?' in *InterMedia*, Vol. 7, No. 4, July 1979.
11. Leonard Marks, *International Conflict and the Free Flow of Information in Control of the Direct Broadcast Satellite, Values in Conflict*, Aspen Institute Program on Communication and Society, Palo Alto, California, 1974, p. 66.
12. Quoted by Kaarle Nordinstreng and Herbert Schiller (eds), National Sovereignty and International Communication, Ablex, New Jersey, 1978.
13. See 'Communication: What Do We Know?' Research Paper No. 9 of the International Commission for the Study of Communication Problems.
14. See Majid Tehranian, 'Iran—Communication, Alienation, Revolution', in *InterMedia*, Vol. 7, No. 2, March 1979, pp. 6–12.
15. Louis A. Perez, Jr., 'Tourism in the West Indies', *Journal of Communication*, Vol. 25, No. 2, 1976, pp. 136–43.
16. Daniel Lerner, *The Passing of Traditional Society*, The Free Press, Glencoe, Illinois, 1958.
17. Ithiel de Sola Pool, 'The Mass Media and Politics in the Modernization Process', in Lucien W. Pye (ed.), *Communications and Political Development*, Princeton University Press, New Jersey, 1963.
18. Lucien W. Pye, ibid.
19. Frederick W. Frey, 'Communication and Development', in Ithiel de Sola Pool and Wilbur Schramm (eds), *Handbook of Communication*, Rand McNally College Publishing Co., Chicago, 1973.
20. See Oliver Boyd-Barrett, *Mass Communications in Cross-Cultural Contexts: The Case of the Third World*, Unit No. 5 of the Open University third-level course in Mass Communication and Society, Open University Press, Milton Keynes, 1977.
21. Antonio Pasquali, 'Mass Media and National Culture—Structure, Content, Values and Impact', *Democratic Journalist*, No. 1, Prague, 1979, pp. 20–1.

22. Elihu Katz and George Wedell, *Broadcasting in the Third World*, Macmillan, London, 1978.
23. Ibid., pp. 23–4.

Chapter 3

1. Quoted by Colin Legum and John Cornwell in their background paper to *A Free and Balanced Flow*, a report of the Twentieth Century Fund Task Force on the International Flow of News, Lexington Books, New York, p. 32.
2. Fernando Reyes Matta, 'The Latin American Concept of News', *Journal of Communication*, Vol. 29, No. 2, Spring 1979, pp. 164–71.
3. Much valuable information on the early development of the wire services is provided in Chapter Two of Phil Harris, op. cit.
4. G. Storey, *Reuter's Century 1851–1951*, Parrish, London, 1951.
5. See Gunnar Naesselund, 'Collaboration between News Agencies in Nordic Countries', Research Document No. 16 of the International Commission for the Study of Communication Problems.
6. George Scott, *Reporter Anonymous—The Story of the Press Association*, Hutchinson, London, 1968.
7. Much information in this section is derived from material collected in the research reports and monographs of the International Commission for the Study of Communication Problems and from Harris, op. cit., as well as from interviews with officials of the various agencies mentioned.
8. The information concerning Third World national news agencies is derived from the reports of those agencies to the International Commission for the Study of Communication Problems.
9. Roger Tatarian, 'News Flow in the Third World—An Overview', in Philip C. Horton (ed.), *The Third World and Press Freedom*, Praeger, New York, 1978, pp. 1–54.
10. Herbert Schiller, op. cit., and Herbert Schiller, 'Communication Accompanies Capital Flows', Research Document No. 47 of the International Commission for the Study of Communication Problems.
11. Jeremy Tunstall, *The Media are American*, Constable, London, 1977.
12. Nordenstreng *et al.*, op. cit.
13. See Michael Schudson, *Discovering the News: A Social History of American Newspapers*, Basic Books, New York, 1978, for an elegant account of these developments in news theory.
14. Gaye Tuchman, 'Objectivity as Strategic Ritual: An Examination of Newsmen's Notions of Objectivity', *American Journal of Sociology*, No. 77, 1972, pp. 660–80.
15. Dilip Mukerjee, 'The World of News Agencies', Research Document No. 11, International Commission for the Study of Communication Problems, p. 19.
16. There exist two privately circulating papers (available through the Free-Flow of News Division of UNESCO) written by the IPS correspondent at Geneva, Chakravarthi Raghavan, which are most instructive in respect of this discussion. One is entitled 'International Reporting of Third World Countries and Issues: Some Annotated Examples'. The other is a background paper for a consultation on 'Responsible, Comprehensive and Objective Reporting of International News', 1979.
17. Christopher A. Nascimento, 'Conflict or a Free and Open Encounter', paper delivered at the annual conference of the International Institute of Communications, London, 1979.
18. Kent Cooper, op. cit., p. 12.
19. Ibid.
20. Narinder Aggarwala, in *Development Forum*, October 1978.

21. *Los Angeles Times*, 10 September 1978.
22. Altaf Gauhar: 'A Destiny Built on the Past', *The Guardian*, 12 February 1979.
23. William A. Dorman and Ehsan Omeed, 'Reporting Iran the Shah's Way', *Columbia Journalism Review*, January/February 1979, pp. 27–33.
24. 6 September 1978, quoted by Dorman and Omeed, ibid.
25. Juan Somavia, *The Transnational Power Structure and International Information*, ILET, Mexico City, 1978, p. 8.
26. Gerald Long, quoted in Research Document No. 13 of the International Commission for the Study of Communication Problems, pp. 122–3.
27. See Edward T. Pinch, 'The Flow of News: An Assessment of the Non-Aligned Agencies Pool', *Journal of Communication*, Vol. 28, No. 4, Autumn 1978, pp. 163–71.
28. *Atlas World Press Review*, New York, December 1977, p. 34.
29. See Pero Ivaçiç: 'The Flow of News: Tanjug, the Pool, and the National Agencies', *Journal of Communication*, Vol. 28, No. 4, Autumn 1978, pp. 157–62.

Chapter 4

1. For further discussion of this, see Rita Cruise O'Brien, 'Specialized Information and Global Interdependence: Problems of Concentration and Access', paper given to annual conference of International Institute of Communications, London, 1979. See also R. Cruise O'Brien and G. K. Helleiner, *The Political Economy of Information in a Changing International Economic Order*, forthcoming.
2. See John Howkins, 'The Management of the Spectrum', *InterMedia*, Vol. 7, No. 5, September 1979, pp. 10–22.
3. Report and Conclusions of the Meeting of Representatives of Telecommunication Administrations of Non-Alligned Countries in Preparation for the WARC, 1979, Yaounde, Cameroon, May 1979.
4. Glen O. Robinson, 'The US Faces WARC', *Journal of Communication*, Vol. 29, No. 1 Winter 1979, pp. 150–7.
5. *Toronto Sunday Star*, 8 July 1979.
6. 'Informatics in the Service of the New International Economic Order', Intergovernmental Bureau of Informatics (IBI), July 1978.
7. Svenson and Wentzel (eds), *The Vulnerable Society*, Swedish Secretariat for Future Studies, Stockholm, 1978.
8. Robert E. Jackson, 'Satellite Business Systems and the Concept of the Dispersed Enterprise: An End to Sovereignty', *Media, Culture and Society*, Vol. 1, No. 3, London, July 1979, pp. 235–53. See also Nancy Foy, *The Sun Never Sets on IBM*, William Morrow and Co., New York, 1975.
9. See Herbert I. Schiller, 'Computer Systems: Power for Whom and for What?' *Journal of Communication*, Vol. 28, No. 4, Autumn 1978, pp. 184–93.
10. *Computerworld*, 3 October 1977.
11. Herbert I. Schiller, 'Computer Systems', op. cit.
12. Remarks of Henry Geller, Assistant Secretary for Communications and Information, before the international conference on Information and Technology, Paris, 27 September 1979. National Telecommunications and Information Administration, Washington, D.C.
13. John Dizard, 'The Revolution in Telecommunications Finance', *Institutional Investor*, September 1979, pp. 146–9. Other facts in this section are also drawn from this most valuable article.
14. Herbert I. Schiller, 'Computer Systems', op. cit.

15. Simon Nora and Alain Minc, op. cit.
16. Mustapha Masmoudi, 'New World Information Order', Document No. 31 presented to the International Commission for the Study of Communications Problems.
17. As reported to the international colloquium, Informatique et Société, Paris, 24–8 September 1979.

Chapter 5

1. Joe Rodrigues, Report of Annual Conference of the IPI, Athens, June 1979.
2. Elihu Katz and George Wedell, *Broadcasting in the Third World*, Macmillan, London, 1978.
3. Neville Jayaweera, 'Political Access to the Media in Sri Lanka', *World Association for Christian Communication (WACC) Journal*, Vol. XXII, No. 1, 1975, pp. 3–6.
4. Shelton A. Gunaratne, 'Media Subservience and Developmental Journalism', *Communications and Development Review*, Vol. 2, No. 2, pp. 3–7.
5. Fred S. Siebert, Theodore Peterson and Wilbur Schramm, *Four Theories of the Press*, University of Illinois Press, Urbana, 1956, 1971.
6. Peter Golding, 'Media Professionalism in the Third World: The Transfer of an Ideology', in James Curran, Michael Gurevitch and Janet Woollacott (eds), *Mass Communication and Society*, Edward Arnold and Open University Press, London, 1977, pp. 291–308.
7. Ibid., p. 297.
8. J. Natarajan, *History of Indian Journalism*, report of the Press Commission, Part II, p. 14.
9. Ibid., pp. 243–7.
10. Kusum Singh, 'Elite Control and Challenge in Changing India', in George Gerbner (ed.), *Mass Media Policies in Changing Cultures*, John Wiley and Sons, New York, 1977, pp. 147–58.
11. P. V. Krishnamoorthy, 'Problems of Communication—the Indian Experience', unpublished paper, Delhi, 1979.
12. Kusum Singh, op. cit.
13. George Verghese, 'Press Censorship under Indira Gandhi', in Philip C. Horton (ed.), *The Third World and Press Freedom*, Praeger, New York, 1978, pp. 220–30.
14. The Press Council Act, 1978, Delhi.
15. See Robert T. Filep and Syed M. S. Hague, 'Communications Development in India', in Majid Tehranian, *et al.* (eds) *Communication Policy for National Development*, Routledge and Kegan Paul, London, 1977, pp. 242–56.
16. B. Mody, 'Social Research and Evaluation of the Satellites Instructional Experiment', Indian Space Research Organization, Ahmedabad, 1974.
17. P. V. Krishnamoorthy, op. cit., p. 13.
18. Altaf Gauhar, 'Free Flow of Information, Myths and Shibboleths', *Third World Quarterly*, Vol. 1, No. 3, July 1979, pp. 13–77.
19. See James W. Carey, 'A Plea for the University Tradition', *Journalism Studies Review*, No. 4, Cardiff, July 1979, pp. 29–31.

Index